THEME -A- SAURUS

The Great Big Book of Mini Teaching Themes

Compiled by **Jean Warren**

Illustrated by **Cora L. Walker**

Warren Publishing House, Inc.
Everett, Washington

Special thanks to Jeannie Lybecker, children's literature specialist, for compiling a list of children's books for each unit. For information about these books or other children's literature, write Ms. Lybecker at Early Childhood Bookhouse, P.O. Box 2791, Portland, OR 97208.

Editor: Gayle Bittinger
Contributing Editor: Elizabeth McKinnon
Consulting Editor: Sue Foster
Assistant Editor: Claudia G. Reid
Layout and Cover Design: Kathy Jones

ISBN 0-911019-20-0

Library of Congress Catalog Number 88-051450
Printed in the United States of America
Published by: Warren Publishing House, Inc.
P.O. Box 2255
Everett, WA 98203

INTRODUCTION

Capture the Moments

Capture the moments
    Follow their lead.
Build on the wonder
    Build on the need.

Look for beginnings
    For reasons to know,
Capture the moments
    And knowledge will grow.

Jean Warren

Each day is filled with unexpected moments — a spider is discovered during a nature walk, a sudden rain shower occurs, you receive a surprise donation of dozens of boxes. Moments such as these provide opportunities for learning, and the ideas in this book will help you take advantage of them. When the first red and gold leaves of autumn appear, you need only turn to the unit on leaves to find a related song to sing or an easy activity to do, right at your fingertips.

Each teaching unit contains a collection of activities from a variety of curriculum areas such as art, science, language, learning games, movement, music and snacks. All of the ideas are developmentally appropriate for young children and use only inexpensive, readily available materials.

Filled with beginnings, *Theme-A-Saurus* will get you going. With this book you will find it easy to build on your children's wonder and excitement and to "capture the moments."

Jean Warren

CONTENTS

CONTENTS

CONTENTS

Print Apples

Set out corks and shallow containers filled with red tempera paint. Give each child an apple tree shape cut out of construction paper. Let the children use the round ends of the corks to print "apples" on their tree shapes. After the paint has dried, use the prints for counting.

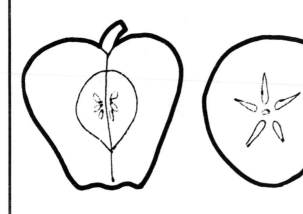

Apple Printing

Cut some apples in half vertically and others in half horizontally. Show the children the hidden star inside the apples cut horizontally. Pour small amounts of red tempera paint onto several sponges set in shallow containers. Let the children dab the apple halves on the sponges and then gently press the apples on pieces of construction paper to make prints.

Apple Collages

Give each child a small paper plate and a piece of red paper. Let the children tear their papers into small pieces. Then have them glue the pieces all over their paper plates. Add green paper stems and use the "apples" as room decorations.

Fingerpaint Apples

Cut large apple shapes out of white butcher paper. Give each child an apple shape and a small amount of red fingerpaint. Let the children paint the apple shapes. Attach precut green leaves to the top of each apple when the shapes have dried.

Observing Changes

Observe and discuss with the children what raw apples look like. Ask them to predict what will happen when the apples are cooked. Bake a whole apple. Slice and simmer another one. Have the children compare the results with the raw apples. Ask them to describe the changes that occurred in color, texture and taste.

Learning Center

Set up an apple activity center. Provide a variety of items for the children to explore such as red, green and yellow apples; apple seeds to examine with a magnifying glass; and foods made with apples (applesauce, dried apples, apple juice).

Comparing Seeds

Have the children use a magnifying glass to look at seeds inside and outside of an apple. Ask them to compare the apple seeds with other fruit seeds that you have set out.

How Many Seeds?

Hold up an apple and ask the children to predict the number of seeds that will be found inside. Cut the apple open and count the seeds with the children. Have them compare the number of seeds with their predictions. Try the experiment with another apple. Does it have the same number of seeds as the first one? Try the same experiment using a different colored apple.

Apple Book

Cut a red construction paper cover and newsprint pages into an apple shape. As a group make a book about apples by having the children each dictate a story for you to record on one of the apple-shaped pages. Let each child illustrate his or her story. Then staple the cover and pages together to make an Apple Book.

Variation: Make a separate book for each child's story.

The Letter ''A''

Introduce the letter ''A'' to the children by showing them the written word ''Apple'' and helping them to see that it begins with an ''A.'' Identify children in your group who have names beginning with ''A.'' Cut a large apple shape out of paper and write the letter ''A'' on it. Have the children tear or cut out magazine pictures of things that have names beginning with ''A'' and then glue the pictures on the apple shape.

Apple Man Puppet

Stick whole cloves into one side of an apple to make two eyes, a nose and a mouth. Stick toothpicks into the apple on either side of the face to make arms. If desired, complete your Apple Man puppet by attaching carrot curls for hair. Let the children take turns making up stories about Apple Man's adventures. Record their stories on tape to listen to again later or write each child's response on paper and let him or her illustrate the story.

Extension: Use your puppet when singing the Apple Man song on page 14.

Apple Counting Game

Glue a felt tree shape to each of five cardboard squares. Write a number from 1 to 5 under each tree. Cut fifteen apple shapes out of felt. To play the game, have the children take turns identifying the numbers below the trees and placing the corresponding number of apples on them.

Apple Colors

Have the children sort different colors of apples (or apple shapes cut from construction paper) into baskets. Let them count how many red, green and yellow apples there are. Then ask them to line up the apples in each group from smallest to largest.

Numbered Apples

Make a felt apple tree and ten felt apples and place the tree on a flannelboard. Number the apples from 1 to 10. Let each child in turn choose an apple, identify the number on it and place the apple on the tree. When all the apples are on the tree, count them as a group.

Do You Know the Apple Man?
Sung to: "The Muffin Man"

Oh, do you know the Apple Man,
The Apple Man,
The Apple Man?
Oh, do you know the Apple Man
Who likes to play with me?

Oh, he has a great big smile,
A great big smile,
A great big smile.
Oh, he has a great big smile
And likes to play with me.

Continue with other verses that the
children make up about Apple Man.

Jean Warren

Applesauce
Sung to: "Yankee Doodle"

Peel an apple,
Cut it up,
Cook it in a pot.
When you taste it
You will find
It's applesauce you've got!

Martha T. Lyon
Fort Wayne, IN

Look at the Apple
Sung to: "The Mulberry Bush"

Look at the apple I have found,
So fat and rosy on the ground.
Mother will wash it and
Cut it in two —
Half for me and half for you.

Martha T. Lyon
Fort Wayne, IN

Apple Coleslaw

In a bowl mix together ¼ cup mayonnaise, ¼ cup milk and 1 teaspoon lemon juice. Grate 1 large apple and 1 small cabbage and add them to the mayonnaise mixture. Makes 8 servings.

Apple Finger Cubes

Pour 2 envelopes unflavored gelatin into a bowl. Add 2 cups boiling water. Stir until gelatin is dissolved. Add one 6-ounce can unsweetened frozen apple juice concentrate. Pour mixture into a lightly greased 9- by 13-inch cake pan and chill. Cut into squares when firm.

Applesauce

Quarter, core and peel 3 to 4 sweet apples. Cut the quarter pieces in half and put them in a saucepan. Add ½ cup water, sprinkle on ½ teaspoon cinnamon and simmer, covered, until the apples are tender (about 20 minutes). Have the children mash the cooked apples with a potato masher or whirl them in a blender. Cool and eat. Makes 6 servings.

Children's Books:
- *Johnny Appleseed*, Steven Kellogg, (Dial, 1988).
- *Rain Makes Applesauce*, Julian Scheer, (Holiday, 1964).
- *Seasons of Arnold's Apple Tree*, Gail Gibbons, (Harcourt, 1984).

Contributors:
Betty Ruth Baker, Waco, TX
Peggy Hanley, St. Joseph, MI
Martha T. Lyon, Fort Wayne, IN
Dawn Picolelli, Wilmington, DE

Fingerprint Balloons

Glue five bottle caps (open ends up) in a semicircle on a piece of heavy cardboard and fill each cap with a different color of tempera paint. Have each child in turn dip all five fingers of one hand into the paint in the bottle caps and then press them on a sheet of white construction paper to make prints. When the paint has dried, let the children draw lines down from their fingerprints, turning them into balloons with strings.

Printing With Balloons

Pour three or four different colors of tempera paint into separate aluminum pie tins. Partially blow up a small balloon that matches each paint color. Then have the children dip the balloons into the matching colored paints and press them on sheets of white construction paper to create balloon prints.

Variation: Use just one color of paint and matching colored balloons.

Balloon Puppets

For each child blow up a balloon until it is about the size of a large cantaloupe. Tie several strands of curled ribbon around the knot to represent hair and attach a loop of ribbon large enough to slip over the child's hand. Then let the children make faces on their balloons by sticking on gummed reinforcement circles. When they have finished, let them wear their balloon puppets on their wrists.

Jet Balloons

While blowing up balloons, let a few of them go before tying them closed and watch them fly around the room. Have the children try to guess why this happens. What makes the balloons go? How far will they go before they stop? How can you make them go again?

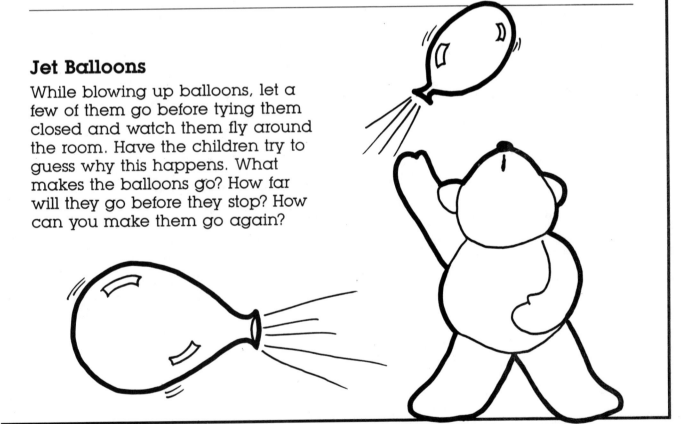

BALLOONS

Magic Balloons

Blow up several balloons. Let the children rub the balloons on their clothes or their hair and place them on a wall. Have the children try guessing what causes the balloons to stay up (static electricity).

Singing Balloon

Blow up a balloon and demonstrate how it "sings" by stretching the opening as you let out the air. Ask the children to tell you whether the air is coming out quickly or slowly. Experiment with different rates of escaping air. Let the children feel the air escaping by placing their hands over the balloon opening.

Balloon Lotto

Make a balloon lotto game by dividing a piece of heavy white paper into six sections and drawing a different colored balloon in each square. Cut matching colored squares out of construction paper. To play the game, have the children take turns placing the construction paper squares on top of the matching colored balloons.

Balloon Fish

Partially blow up ten small balloons. Place them in a dishpan full of water. Set the pan on the floor and let the children take turns fishing for balloon fish with a wire food strainer. Help each child count his or her catch before putting the fish back in the pan.

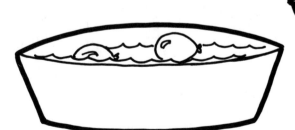

BALLOONS

Balloon Jump

Blow up balloons and tie them with long strings. Then hang the balloons from the ceiling at a height that will tempt the children to stretch, jump and bat the balloons around.

Popping Balloons

Let the children help you pretend to blow up balloons and fill the room with them. Then have them pretend to tape sharp pins on their knees and elbows so that they can "pop" the balloons. Encourage them to reach their knees and elbows way up high and way down low until all of the balloons have popped.

Balloon in the Air

Stand in a group with the children and tap up a balloon. (Use two or three balloons for a large group.) Have the child closest to where the balloon starts to come down tap it up again with his or her hand. The object of the game is to see how long the group can keep the balloon in the air.

Creative Movement Fun

Let the children watch you blow up a balloon and then slowly deflate it. Have them pretend that they are limp balloons, expanding as they breathe air in and whistling as they let air out. Let the children spin and dash around like balloons that have been inflated and released. Or let them pretend to be inflated balloons floating lazily about the room while gently bumping into things.

BALLOONS

Bounce the Balloons
Sung to: ''The Mulberry Bush''

This is the way we
Bounce the balloons,
Bounce the balloons,
Bounce the balloons.
This is the way we
Bounce the balloons,
Gently in the air.

Joyce Marshall
Whitby, Ontario

Balloon Song
Sung to: ''Ten Little Indians''

One little, two little,
Three little balloons,
Four little, five little,
Six little balloons.
Seven little, eight little,
Nine little balloons,
Floating up so high.

Joyce Marshall
Whitby, Ontario

Red Balloons
Sung to: ''Frere Jacques''

Red balloons, red balloons,
Floating up, floating up.
Never let them touch the ground,
Never let them touch the ground.
Keep them up. Keep them up.

Repeat, letting the children suggest other
balloon colors.

Joyce Marshall
Whitby, Ontario

My Balloon
Sung to: "Pop! Goes the Weasel"

Here I have a big balloon,
Watch me while I blow.
Small at first, then bigger,
   (Make circles with thumbs and fingers.)
Watch it grow and grow.
   (Make bigger and bigger circles
with arms.)

Do you think it's big enough?
Maybe I should stop.
For if I blow much longer,
My balloon will pop!

Adapted Traditional

Children's Books:
- *Balloon Trip*, Ron Wegen,
  (Houghton Mifflin, 1981).
- *Belinda's Balloon*, Emilie Boon,
  (Knopf, 1985).
- *Hot-Air Henry*, Mary Calhoun,
  (Morrow, 1981).

Balloon Treats
Write each child's name on a
balloon and tie it to the back of his
or her chair before snacktime. For
balloon snacks, serve such foods
as round crackers, carrot slices,
banana slices, orange slices, egg
slices or cucumber slices.

Contributors:
Lena Goehring, Columbus, PA
Joyce Marshall, Whitby, Ontario

Lacing Bear Shapes

Cut brown posterboard into bear shapes and punch holes around the edges. Give each child a bear shape and a piece of colorful yarn with one end taped to make a "needle." Then let the children lace the yarn through the holes.

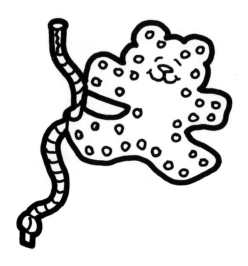

Teddy Bear Puppets

Have the children use brown lunch bags to make simple teddy bear hand puppets. Let them create faces on their puppets by gluing on scraps of construction paper and drawing with felt-tip markers. Add two brown ear shapes to each puppet.

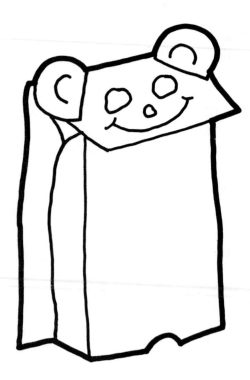

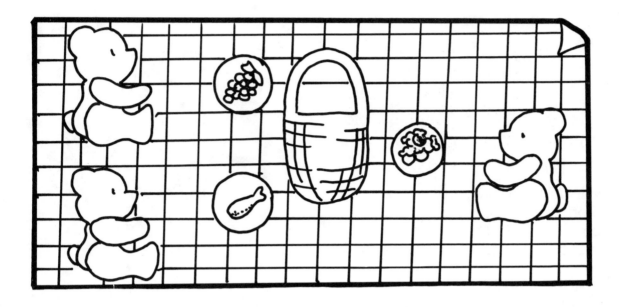

Teddy Bears' Picnic

Give each child a sitting bear shape cut out of brown construction paper. Have the children brush their bear shapes with a thin layer of glue. Then let them sprinkle coffee grounds (rinsed and dried) all over the glue and shake off the excess. Set the bear shapes aside to dry. Give each child a small paper plate. Let the children glue precut pictures of foods on their plates to make picnic lunches. Hang a red and white checkered tablecloth on a wall or a bulletin board. Attach the bear shapes to the tablecloth, with each bear holding a plate. If desired, add other shapes cut out of construction paper, such as a picnic basket, a shade tree, a sun and grass.

Weighing Bears

Review the concepts of heavy and light by having one child at a time hold a different teddy bear in each hand. Which bear feels heavier? Which feels lighter? Or let the children use a balance to compare the weights of different teddy bears.

Teddy Bear Games

Collect a large group of teddy bears before playing the games below.

Let the children count the total number of teddy bears.

Ask the children to sort the teddy bears by categories (color, size, those wearing bows, etc.). Then have them count the number of bears in each category.

Have the children make different sets of teddy bears (five brown bears, three white bears, etc.).

The Three Bears

Read the story "The Three Bears" to the children. After you have finished, set out several sets of three objects in small, medium and large sizes, such as three bowls, three spoons, three cups and three plates. Have the children divide the objects into three piles, one for the Papa Bear, one for the Mama Bear and one for the Baby Bear (in that order). When the objects have been grouped according to size, have the children regroup them into piles of like objects.

Teddy Bear Book

Let the children dictate stories about teddy bears while you write them down. (This could be a small group activity or each child could dictate his or her own story.) Have the children illustrate their stories. Then staple them together with a cover to make a Teddy Bear Book.

ABC Bears

Cut 26 teddy bear shapes out of posterboard and write the letters "A" through "Z" on them with a felt-tip marker. Laminate or cover each bear with clear self-stick paper. Then mix up the bears and let the children have fun arranging them in alphabetical order.

Here Is a Cave

Read the poem below and let the
children make the appropriate
finger movements.

Here is a cave.
  (Bend fingers on one hand.)
Inside is a bear.
  (Put thumb inside fingers.)
Now he comes out
To get some fresh air.
  (Pop out thumb.)

He stays out all summer
In sunshine and heat.
He hunts in the forest
For berries to eat.
  (Move thumb in a circle.)

When snow starts to fall,
He hurries inside
His warm little cave
And there he will hide.
  (Put thumb inside fingers.)

Snow covers the cave
Like a fluffy white rug.
Inside the bear sleeps
All cozy and snug.
  (Place one hand over the other.)

Author Unknown

Teddy Bear Parade

Give each child a box with a rope pull-handle. Let the children decorate their boxes with crepe paper streamers. When the boxes are decorated, have the children place teddy bears inside. Then play music and let the children pull their boxes around the room in a Teddy Bear Parade.

Bear Bounce

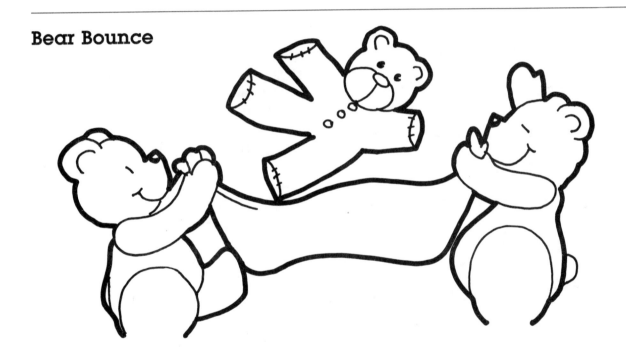

Place a small blanket on the floor with a teddy bear in the middle. Have two children each grab two corners of the blanket. Then let them have fun tossing and catching the bear with the blanket.

Teddy Bear, Teddy Bear

As you recite the rhyme below, let the children pretend to be teddy bears and act out the movements.

Teddy bear, teddy bear, turn around,
Teddy bear, teddy bear, touch the ground.
Teddy bear, teddy bear, reach up high,
Teddy bear, teddy bear, touch the sky.
Teddy bear, teddy bear, touch your shoe,
Teddy bear, teddy bear, I love you!

Traditional

Variation: Let the children use teddy bears as puppets to act out the movements.

Three Brown Bears

Sung to: ``Three Blind Mice''

Three brown bears,
Three brown bears.
See all their beds,
See all their chairs.
The mommy cooked in
A big brown pot,
The daddy's porridge
Was much too hot,
The baby bear
Always cried a lot,
Three brown bears.

Judith McNitt
Adrian, MI

Peanut Butter Bear Sandwiches

Have the children use a valentine cookie cutter to cut heart shapes out of whole-wheat bread slices (partially frozen bread cuts easily). Show them how to cut off the points of their hearts to make the bread resemble bear faces. Then let each child spread peanut butter on his or her bear face and use raisins to make eyes and a mouth and a cherry to make a nose.

Bear Cookies

Make or buy bear-shaped cookies. Let the children decorate the cookies with white frosting for polar bears, brown frosting for brown bears, black frosting for black bears and black and white frosting for panda bears. (Check a local bakery to find out where you can purchase black food coloring paste.)

Children's Books:
- *Jesse Bear, What Will You Wear?*, Nancy Carlstrom, (Macmillan, 1986).
- *Peace at Last*, Jill Murphy, (Dial, 1980).
- *Teddy Bears' Picnic*, Jimmy Kennedy, (Green Tiger, 1983).

Contributors:
Joyce Marshall, Whitby, Ontario
Judith McNitt, Adrian, MI
Nancy C. Windes, Denver, CO

Musical Drawings

Provide the children with large pieces of paper and crayons or felt-tip markers. Play the classical piece "The Flight of the Bumblebee" by Rimsky-Korsakov. Encourage the children to think of their crayons or markers as "bees" as they draw to the music.

Bees in Honeycombs

Cut empty toilet tissue tubes and paper towel tubes into sections of varying lengths. Let the children make honeycombs by paper-clipping or gluing sections of tubes together, side-to-side. Then have the children make bees, using playdough for bodies and pepper-corns for eyes. Bake the playdough bees at 250 degrees for about an hour, depending on their sizes. Let the children glue their bees to their honeycombs.

Balloon Bees

Blow up a yellow balloon for each child. Let the children use their balloons to make "bees" by drawing stripes around them with black felt-tip markers. If desired, have the children add circle stickers for eyes (or have them draw eyes on their bees with the markers). When the children have finished, let them tap their balloon bees up and down in the air as they "buzz" around the room.

Bumblebee on My Nose
Sung to: "Jingle Bells"

Bumblebee, bumblebee,
Landing on my toes.
Bumblebee, bumblebee,
Now he's on my nose.
On my arms, on my legs,
On my elbows.
Bumblebee, oh, bumblebee,
He lands and then he goes!

Jean Warren

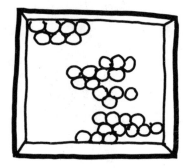

Honeycomb Observation

Bring in a real honeycomb for the children to examine. Explain that a honeycomb is made out of wax that the bees make with their bodies. The honeycomb serves as a nest for the bees and as a place for storing their honey.

"B"Hive Game

Cover a small box with brown paper to make a beehive. Cut a slit in the top of the beehive and label it with the letter "B." Cut bee shapes out of construction paper. Glue pictures of things that have names beginning with "B" and pictures of things that have names beginning with other letters on the bee shapes. Explain to the children that only the bees that have pictures of things whose names begin with "B" can go into the "B"hive. Then let the children take turns selecting a bee and deciding whether or not it can go into the beehive.

Here Is the Beehive

Cut a beehive shape and five bee
shapes out of felt. Attach the bees
in a column to a piece of yarn or
fishing line and place them on a
flannelboard. Before you recite the
poem below, place the beehive
over the bee column, leaving the
top of the piece of yarn exposed.
Then read the poem. As you begin
counting, slowly pull the bees out
of the beehive, one at a time.

Here is the beehive.
Where are the bees?
Hidden away where nobody sees.
Here they come buzzing
Out of the hive —
One, two, three, four and five!

Traditional

Buzzing Game

Select two children to be searchers.
Have them leave the room while
you and the other children hide an
object. When the searchers return,
have the other children start
buzzing. The closer the searchers
get to the hidden object, the
louder the others should buzz. The
farther away the searchers get, the
softer the others should buzz. When
the object is found, select two more
children to be the searchers.

Bee Stripes

Cut five pairs of bee shapes out of construction paper. On each pair draw one, two, three, four or five stripes. If desired, laminate the shapes or cover them with clear self-stick paper for durability. Challenge the children to find each pair of bees by matching or counting the stripes.

Bees in the Beehive

Divide the children into groups of threes. Have two of the children in each group hold hands to form a "beehive." Have the third child stand inside the beehive as a "bee." When a signal sounds, have the bees run to find new hives. Repeat the action, letting the children take turns being hives and bees.

Beehive Story

Cut several bee shapes and a beehive shape out of felt. Place the shapes on a flannelboard. Make up a story about the bees that involves adding and subtracting. Add and remove the bee shapes as you tell the story. For example: "Let's peek into the hive this morning and count the bees. Two are leaving to look for flowers. How many are left in the hive?"

A Taste of Honey

Put small amounts of honey into paper cups and add sesame seeds. Then let the children dip carrot sticks, apple slices or orange segments into the honey for a sweet "bee snack."

Children's Books:
- *Bumble Bee*, Barrie Watts, (Silver Burdett, 1987).
- *The Reason for a Flower*, Ruth Heller, (Putnam, 1983).
- *Rose in My Garden*, Arnold Lobel, (Greenwillow, 1984).

Contributors:
Colraine Pettipaw Hunley, Doylestown, PA
Betty Silkunas, Lansdale, PA
Carolyn Tyson, Ann Arbor, MI

Egg Cup Bells

Cut out the egg cups from cardboard egg cartons. Place newspapers on a table and give each child several egg cups, some tempera paint and a small brush. Let the children paint their egg cups, first on the inside and then on the outside. When the paint has dried, poke pipe cleaners through the centers of the cups. Make a hook out of the top half of each pipe cleaner and roll the bottom half up inside the cup to make a bell clapper.

Variation: Before inserting the pipe cleaners, have the children dip the rims of their painted egg cups into glue, then into silver glitter.

Sound Discrimination

Let the children play with different kinds of bells (sleigh bells, dinner bells, cow bells, bird cage bells, etc.). Encourage them to listen to the unique sound each bell makes. Help them decide on a name to distinguish each bell. Then play a game with the children. Have them close their eyes while you ring one of the bells. When they open their eyes, ask them to point to and name the bell they think you just rang.

Bell Bracelets

To make each bell bracelet, string a large pipe cleaner with three to four bells and twist it into a bracelet shape. (A ¼-inch wide ribbon can be used in place of a pipe cleaner.) Let the children play their bell bracelets by putting them on their wrists and shaking their hands up and down.

Bell Mitts

Make hand mitts out of cotton fabric or felt (or use old knit mittens). Sew two bells on the top of each mitt. Let the children play their bell mitts by putting them on and clapping their hands together.

Bells on Poles

For each child string three or four bells together with yarn. Knot one end and let it hang free. Tape the other end to a dowel. Let the children play their bells by shaking their dowels or by tapping them with their hands.

Count the Rings

Number ten index cards from 1 to 10. Give each child a bell. Let the children practice ringing their bells. Then hold up one of the numbered cards. Ask the children to identify the number on the card and have them count as they ring their bells that many times.

Bell Ring

Hang a bell up high. Give the children beanbags (or socks rolled into balls). Then let them take turns tossing the beanbags at the bell to make it ring.

Ring the Bells
Sung to: ''This Old Man''

Ring, ring, ring the bells,
Ring them all around.
Ring them loud
Then ring them soft.
Now don't make a sound.

Jean Warren

Jingle All the Way
Sung to: ''Jingle Bells''

Jingle bells, jingle bells,
Jingle all the way.
Oh, what fun it is to play
My jingle bells today.
Shake them fast, shake them slow,
Shake them loud and clear.
Oh, what fun it is to shake
My bells for all to hear.

Jean Warren

Children's Books:
- *Jingle Bear*, Stephen Cosgrove, (Price Stern Sloan, 1985).
- *Over the River and Through the Wood*, Lydia Child, (Scholastic, 1987).
- *Polar Express*, Chris Van Allsburg, (Houghton Mifflin, 1985).

Circle Birds

Give each child a 4½-inch circle and a 2½-inch circle cut out of light blue construction paper. Have the children glue their circles on pieces of dark blue construction paper, using the large circles for bodies and the small circles for heads. Then let them decorate their circle birds with felt-tip markers and feathers.

Feather Painting

Set out tempera paint, feathers and pieces of construction paper. Let the children experiment with using the feathers as paint brushes. Encourage them to make as many different patterns and lines as they can with their feathers.

Five Little Bluebirds

Cut five bluebird shapes out of felt. As you recite the poem below, place the bird shapes on a flannelboard.

Five little bluebirds waiting for spring —

The first little bluebird began to sing.
The second little bluebird flapped its wings.
The third little bluebird said,
    ''Tweet, tweet, tweet.''
The fourth little bluebird sang so sweet.
The fifth little bluebird said,
    ''It's a beautiful day.''
Then all five bluebirds flew away.

Betty Ruth Baker
Waco, TX

Winter Treats

Help the children make these winter treats for birds.

Orange or Grapefruit Cup – Punch four holes near the top of an empty orange or grapefruit rind. Attach it to a tree limb with string. Fill the rind with seeds or nuts.

Bread Ornament – Cut a slice of stale bread into a circle or other shape with a cookie cutter. Mix food coloring with hardened fat and spread it on both sides of the bread. Make a hole near the top of the shape and tie it to a tree limb with string.

Suet Bag – Cut a 6-inch square of net from a potato or onion bag. Mix suet with birdseed and place a large spoonful of the mixture in the center of the netting. Bring the corners of the square together and tie with a string. Then fasten the suet bag to a tree branch.

Birds' Nests

Give the children small paper sacks. Then take the children on a walk and let them collect items that a bird might use to make a nest, such as twigs, leaves, grass and pieces of string. After the walk, have the children fold down the sides of their bags to form "nests." Have them set their bags outside so that the birds can use the contents for nest building.

BIRDS

What Am I?
Sung to: "This Old Man"

I am bright, I am red,
I have a crest upon my head.
If you can guess me,
Hurry up and try,
Before I fly into the sky!
(What am I?. . . Cardinal)

I am big, I am blue,
I love oaks and acorns, too.
If you can guess me,
Hurry up and try,
Before I fly into the sky!
(What am I?. . . Bluejay)

I am small, with a black head,
I come in winter to be fed.
If you can guess me,
Hurry up and try,
Before I fly into the sky!
(What am I?. . . Chickadee)

I am tiny, I am fast,
Not many people see me pass.
If you can guess me,
Hurry up and try,
Before I fly into the sky!
(What am I?. . . Hummingbird)

I am big, I am grand,
I'm the bird of our great land.
If you can guess me,
Hurry up and try,
Before I fly into the sky!
(What am I?. . . Bald Eagle)

I am old, I am wise,
I like to hunt before sunrise.
If you can guess me,
Hurry up and try,
Before I fly into the sky!
(What am I?. . . Owl)

I eat bugs, I eat bees,
I live in holes and peck on trees.
If you can guess me,
Hurry up and try,
Before I fly into the sky!
(What am I?. . . Woodpecker)

I am brown, with a red breast,
I come first in spring to nest.
If you can guess me,
Hurry up and try,
Before I fly into the sky!
(What am I?. . . Robin)

Barbara Dunn
Hollidaysburg, PA

Nest Game

From construction paper cut out five nest shapes, five bird shapes and fifteen egg shapes. Glue from one to five eggs inside each nest. Number the birds from 1 to 5. To play the game, have the children help the mother birds find their nests by matching the number of eggs in a nest to the bird with that number written on it.

Bird's Nest Salads

Cut carrots in half and let the children help grate them. For each serving, mix together one half of a grated carrot and ¼ cup chow mein noodles. Stir in mayonnaise to moisten. Place the mixture on a plate and push the back of a spoon down into the middle to form a "nest." Let the children place grapes or peas in their nests for "eggs." If desired, serve the nests on top of lettuce leaves.

Children's Books:
- *Cat and Canary*, Michael Foreman, (Dial, 1985).
- *Tico and the Golden Wings*, Leo Lionni, (Knopf, 1987).
- *Are You My Mother?*, P.D. Eastman, (Random House, 1960).

Contributors:
Marlene Filsinger, Snyder, NY
Joleen Meier, Marietta, GA
Susan M. Paprocki, Northbrook, IL

Treasure Boxes

Let the children personalize boxes for holding treasures. Give each child a box with a lid. Have the children glue collage materials such as buttons, ribbon, fabric and paper scraps, yarn, pasta, glitter or feathers to their boxes to make them extra special.

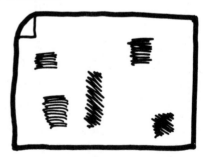

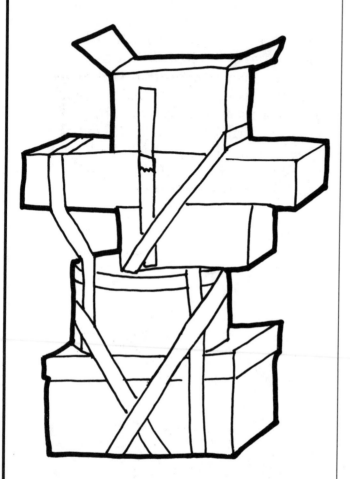

Box Sculpture

Collect boxes in a variety of sizes. Set out the boxes along with some tape and some glue. Let the children work together as a group to create a large sculpture by gluing and taping the boxes together.

Box Prints

Let the children dip the lids of small gift boxes into tempera paint. Then have them press the lids on construction paper to make box prints.

What's in the Box?

Put a surprise object in a shoebox with a lid. Have the children pass the box around and try to guess what's inside. Give clues about the object until someone guesses correctly.

Variation: Each day have a child bring in a box with an object inside. Let the child give clues until the other children guess what's inside.

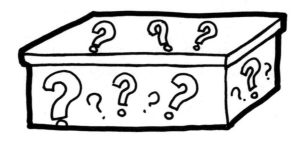

Smaller Than

Select a box of any size and show it to the children. Have each child find something nearby that is smaller than the box and put it inside.

Where's the Box?

Give each child a box. Then have the children follow directions such as these: "Put your box under your chair; Hold your box above your head; Place your box under your arm."

Variation: Put a box in a specific place and ask the children to tell you where it is.

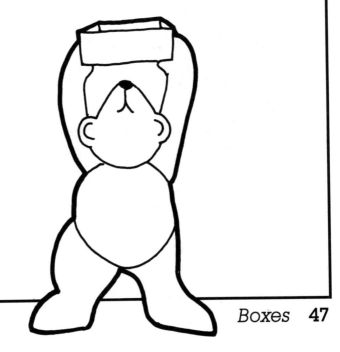

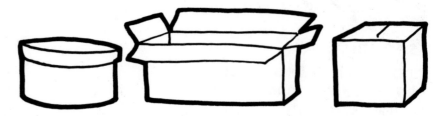

Sorting Game

Set out a round box (such as an oatmeal box), a square box and a rectangular box, along with small objects that are round, square and rectangular. To play the game, have the children choose objects one at a time and place them in the matching shaped boxes.

Contents and Boxes

Set out boxes and the items that belong inside (a toothbrush box and a toothbrush, a film box and a film can, a shoebox and a pair of shoes, etc.). Let the children put the items into the correct boxes.

Matching Lids and Boxes

Place a variety of boxes and lids on a table. Have the children match the lids to the corresponding boxes.

Nesting Boxes

Find boxes that will fit inside each other in a nesting fashion. (Heart-shaped candy boxes are available in many sizes.) Have the children nest the boxes one inside the other or line them up from smallest to largest.

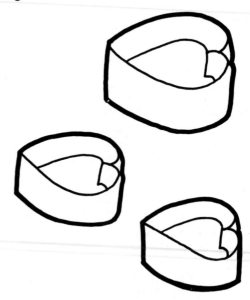

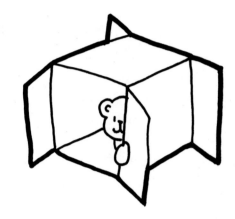

Lifting and Carrying

Have the children act out lifting and carrying boxes that are large and small, heavy and light. Tell the children to fill their imaginary boxes with cotton balls, bricks, etc. Have the children pretend to fill one box that is so big that everyone must help lift and carry it across the room.

Obstacle Course

Arrange sturdy cardboard boxes for the children to climb around and over. Open both ends of a box to make a tunnel. Place a series of boxes together to make steps.

Picnic Box Snacks

For each child pack a snack (or lunch) in a "picnic box." (You may want to include one of the many fruit juices that are packaged in small boxes with straws attached.) Spread a tablecloth on the grass outdoors or on the floor indoors and enjoy a picnic treat.

Children's Books:
- *Boxes! Boxes!*, Leonard Fisher, (Viking, 1984).
- *Christina Katerina and the Box*, Patricia Gauch, (Putnam, 1980).

Contributors:
Susan A. Miller, Kutztown, PA
Donna Mullennix, Thousand Oaks, CA

Blowing Bubbles

Mix together ¼ cup liquid detergent, ½ cup water, a few drops of food coloring and 1 teaspoon sugar. Pour into a shallow container and use with the bubble blowers below.

Ask the children to compare the bubbles made from the different blowers.

Hint: Let the bubble solution age for a few days to make bubble blowing easier.

○ Poke holes in the bottoms of paper cups. Have the children dip the rims of the cups into the bubble solution and blow through the holes.

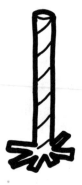

○ Make 1-inch slits on the ends of straws. Bend the strips back. Have the children dip the bent ends of the straws into the bubble solution and blow through the other ends.

○ Tape four to six straws together in a bundle for each child. Have the children dip one of the ends of the straw bundles into the bubble solution and blow through the other ends.

Bubble Prints

In a small margarine tub mix one part liquid tempera paint with two parts liquid dishwashing detergent and stir in a small amount of water. (If you wish to use several colors, make a separate solution for each one.) Let one child at a time put a straw into the paint mixture and blow through it until the bubbles rise above the rim of the margarine tub. Then lay a piece of white paper on top of the bubbles and let the child rub across it gently. As the bubbles break, they will leave delicate prints on the paper. Try various kinds of paper for different results.

Hint: To prevent the children from accidentally sucking up the paint mixture, poke holes near the tops of the straws.

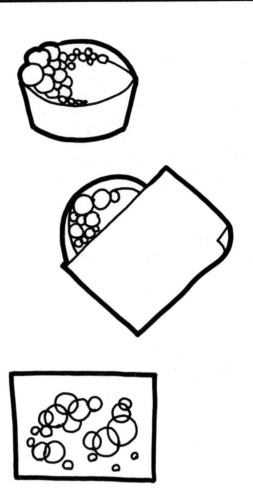

Counting Bubbles

Let the children take turns blowing all the bubbles they can with one breath. Have the rest of the children count the bubbles.

Rainbow Bubbles

Have the children blow bubbles and look at them closely. When the reflection from the sun hits the bubbles, a rainbow of colors can be seen. Ask the children to look for the different colors and name the ones that they see.

Bubble Games

When blowing bubbles with the children, reinforce the concepts of big, little, few, many, high and low. Ask questions such as these: "Can you blow big bubbles? Little bubbles? A few bubbles? Many bubbles? Can you blow your bubbles high in the air? Can you blow them down low?"

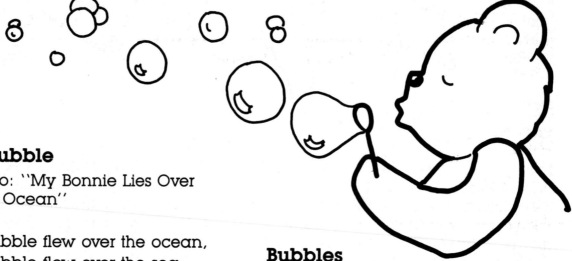

My Bubble

Sung to: "My Bonnie Lies Over the Ocean"

My bubble flew over the ocean,
My bubble flew over the sea.
My bubble flew over the rainbow,
Oh, come back, my bubble,
    to me.
Come back, come back,
Oh, come back, my bubble,
    to me, to me.
Come back, come back,
Oh, come back, my bubble,
    to me.

Jean Warren

Bubbles

Sung to: "Frere Jacques"

Blowing bubbles, blowing bubbles
Is such fun, is such fun.
Blow them everywhere,
See them floating in the air.
Blowing bubbles, blowing bubbles.

Betty Silkunas
Lansdale, PA

Floating Bubbles

Let the children pretend to be bubbles. Play soft music and have them "float" like bubbles around the room.

Orange Fluff

Pour ¼ cup water into a bowl and add 2 envelopes unflavored gelatin. Stir and let set for 5 minutes. Add ¾ cup boiling water and stir again until gelatin is dissolved. Pour mixture into a blender container and add one 6-ounce can unsweetened frozen orange juice concentrate. Blend until fluffy, then pour into small cups. Chill for about 15 minutes. Makes 4 to 6 servings.

Children's Books:
- *Bubble Bubble*, Mercer Mayer, (Macmillan, 1980).
- *The Magic Bubble Trip*, Ingrid and Dieter Schubert, (Kane Miller, 1985).

Bubbly Punch

In a large pitcher mix together one 12-ounce can unsweetened frozen apple juice concentrate, 2 cans (24 ounces) cold water and one 32-ounce bottle club soda. Stir well and pour into plastic glasses. Makes 17 small servings.

Contributors:
Maxine E. Pincott, Windsor, CT
Judith McNitt, Adrian, MI

BUNNIES

Fluffy Bunnies

Give each child a bunny shape cut out of construction paper. Have the children pull cotton pillow stuffing or cotton balls into soft, fluffy pieces and glue them all over their bunny shapes. From pink construction paper cut out ear shapes that are slightly smaller than the ears on the bunnies and cut circles for eyes out of blue construction paper. Then let the children glue the ears and eyes on their cotton bunnies.

Bunny Parade

For each child cut a bunny shape 12 to 16 inches tall out of white construction paper and a large brimmed hat shape out of yellow construction paper. Set the bunny shapes aside and give each child a hat shape. Let the children decorate their hats with any of the following items: straw flowers, ribbon, rickrack, feathers, buttons, stickers, old costume jewelry or sequins. Glue each child's hat to a bunny shape. When the glue has dried, hang the bunnies on a wall to create a ''Bunny Parade.''

Bunny Foods

Discuss with the children the foods that bunnies like to eat (carrots, beets, turnips, barley, oats and fresh-cut clover and grass). Then draw (or cut out of magazines) pictures of foods that bunnies like and pictures of foods that bunnies don't like. Let the children take turns sorting the pictures into two groups.

Textured Bunnies

Draw the outline of a bunny shape on each of twelve index cards and divide the cards into pairs. On each pair glue bunny tail shapes made from the same kind of textured material (sandpaper, cotton balls, velvet, corduroy, etc.). Mix up the cards and let the children take turns matching the bunnies by the textures of their tails.

This Little Bunny

Cut five bunny shapes out of felt and decorate them as described in the following poem. As you recite the poem, place the appropriate shapes on a flannelboard.

This little bunny has two pink eyes,
This little bunny is very wise.
This little bunny is soft as silk,
This little bunny is white as milk.
This little bunny nibbles away
At cabbages and carrots
    the livelong day!

Author Unknown

Bunny Hop-Along

Let one child begin by rolling a large die and calling out the number that comes up. (For very young children, have an adult call out the numbers.) Then have the child hop that number of times while the other children try to follow. Let the child try hopping in various ways (forward, backward, to the side or around in circles). Encourage big hops and little hops. Continue the game until everyone has had a turn being the leader.

Bunny-Pokey

Sung to: "Hokey-Pokey"

You put your bunny ears in,
  (Place hands on head to make "ears.")
You put your bunny ears out,
You put your bunny ears in,
And you shake them all about.
You do the Bunny-Pokey,
And you hop yourself around —
That's what it's all about!

Additional verses: "You put your bunny nose in; You put your bunny tail in; You put your bunny paws in."

Betty Silkunas
Lansdale, PA

Did You Ever See a Bunny?

Sung to: "Did You Ever See a Lassie?"

Did you ever see a bunny,
A bunny, a bunny,
Did you ever see a bunny
That hops so slow?
It hops and hops
And hops and hops.
Did you ever see a bunny
That hops so slow?

Additional verses: "Did you ever see a bunny that hops so fast; that hops backward; that hops on one foot?"

Jean Warren

Egg Bunnies

Boil and peel eggs (at least one for every two children). Slice the eggs in half and show the children how to scoop out the yolks. Mix all the yolks with mayonnaise and let the children help spoon the mixture back into the whites. Then have the children place raisins on their egg halves for bunny eyes and noses and carefully poke 2-inch celery sticks (cut like matchsticks) into the tops of their bunny heads for ears.

Pear Bunnies

For each child place a pear half (flat side down) on a lettuce leaf. In the narrow end of the pear, insert whole cloves for eyes and almond halves for ears. At the other end of the pear, place a spoonful of cottage cheese for a fluffy tail.

Note: Have the children remove the cloves before eating their pear bunnies.

Children's Books:
- *Huge Harold,* Bill Peet, (Houghton Mifflin, 1961).
- *Mr. Rabbit and the Lovely Present,* Charlotte Zolotow, (Harper Row, 1977).
- *Runaway Bunny,* Margaret Wise Brown, (Harper Row, 1972).

Contributors:
Judith Hanson, Newton Falls, OH
Betty Silkunas, Lansdale, PA
Jane M. Spannbauer, South St. Paul, MN

Tissue Paper Butterflies

Cut butterfly shapes from white construction paper. Set out assorted colors of 1-inch tissue paper squares, small containers of water and paintbrushes. Have the children paint the butterfly shapes with water and place the tissue paper squares randomly on the shapes. Have them count to ten, then remove the wet tissue paper to view their colorful creations.

Clothespin Butterflies

Cut various colors of tissue paper into 12-inch squares. Set out slot-type clothespins, colored pipe cleaners and assorted felt-tip markers. Have the children pinch their tissue squares together in the middle and then insert the tissue into the slots of their clothespins to make wings. Have them wind pipe cleaners around the heads of their clothespins, leaving two small ends sticking up to form antennae. Let the children use felt-tip markers to color on eyes and to draw designs on the clothespin bodies of their butterflies. Then tie the butterflies to lengths of fishing line or string and hang them from the ceiling or in a window.

Ink Blot Butterflies

Spread newspapers on a table. Set out tempera paints in individual containers with an eyedropper in each. Let the children use the eyedroppers to drop paint onto pieces of drawing paper and help them fold the papers in half. Have the children press and smooth their papers, then unfold them to reveal the designs they have made. When the paint has dried, cut the papers into butterfly shapes.

Butterfly Match-Ups

Cut three paper plates into four sections each to make six pairs of butterfly wings. Draw from one to six circles on each pair of wings. Cut 3-inch slits in opposite sides of each of six empty toilet tissue tubes. Give the children the butterfly wings and empty tubes. Let them take turns finding matching pairs of wings and inserting them in the slits to make butterflies.

Variation: Make wings for matching colors, shapes, patterns or alphabet letters.

The Life of a Butterfly
Sung to: "Skip to My Lou"

I'm a caterpillar, wiggle with me,
　(Wiggle body.)
I'm a caterpillar, wiggle with me.
I'm a caterpillar, wiggle with me.
What'll I be, my darlin'?

A chrysalis, now sleep like me,
　(Hold arms in a circle above head.)
A chrysalis, now sleep like me.
A chrysalis, now sleep like me.
What'll I be, my darlin'?

A butterfly, come fly with me.
　(Wave arms like wings.)
A butterfly, come fly with me.
A butterfly, come fly with me.
Come fly with me, my darlin'.

Now all together, let's do all three.
A caterpillar, a chrysalis,
　a butterfly — three.
　(Make all three movements.)
Move your body like this with me.
　(Continue waving arms.)
The life of a butterfly, darlin'.

Judy Hall
Wytheville, VA

BUTTERFLIES

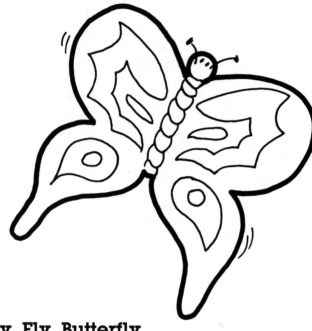

Pretty Butterfly

Sung to: "Up on the Housetop"

First comes a butterfly
Who lays an egg.
Out comes a caterpillar
With many legs.
Oh, see the caterpillar
Spin and spin
A little chrysalis to sleep in.
Oh, oh, oh, look and see,
Oh, oh, oh, look and see.
Out of the chrysalis, my oh, my,
Out comes a pretty butterfly!

Stella Waldron
Lincoln, NE

Fly, Fly, Butterfly

Sung to: "Skip to My Lou"

Fly, fly, butterfly,
Fly, fly, butterfly,
Fly, fly, butterfly.
Fly up in the sky so high.

Flitter, flitter, butterfly,
Flitter, flitter, butterfly,
Flitter, flitter, butterfly.
Flitter and fly up in the sky.

Oh my, butterfly,
Oh my, butterfly,
Oh my, butterfly,
Do you always fly so high?

Jean Warren

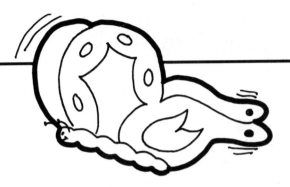

The Butterfly

Read the following story to the children.

One warm day, a caterpillar crawled up into a tree to take a nap on one of the cool green leaves. First she curled up on the leaf and spun a web around herself. In this cozy coverlet, called a "chrysalis," she slept and slept.

When the caterpillar woke up, she crawled out of her chrysalis. But suddenly she realized she no longer had her many legs. How would she ever get home?

The caterpillar started to cry. Then as she tried to wipe away her tears, she discovered, to her joy, that while asleep she had grown two beautiful butterfly wings. She opened her wings, waved them up and down and was soon soaring through the sky.

Ask the children to help you finish the story. Where does the butterfly go? What happens to her? How does the story end?

Sandwich Butterflies

Make sandwiches and cut them into triangles. For each child place a pickle wedge in the center of a plate for a butterfly body. Then place a triangular sandwich on either side of the pickle for wings.

Children's Books:
- *Butterfly and Caterpillar*, Barrie Watts, (Silver Burdett, 1986).
- *Where Does the Butterfly Go When It Rains?*, May Garelick, (Scholastic, 1970).

Contributors:
Paula Schneider, Kent, WA
Vicki Shannon, Napton, MO
Jane M. Spannbauer, South St. Paul, MN

BUTTONS

Button Rings

Set out pipe cleaners and buttons with shanks. Have each child select a button and string a pipe cleaner through its shank. Then help the child wrap his or her button ring around a finger. Let the children make and wear as many rings as they want.

Button Pictures

For each child glue buttons on a piece of construction paper. Hand out the papers along with felt-tip markers or crayons. Let the children draw pictures on their papers and encourage them to use the buttons as part of their pictures. For example, a button could represent a flower, a tire or the sun.

Counting Buttons

Give each child a small pile of buttons. Select a number and have the children count out that number of buttons from their piles. Repeat, using numbers the children are familiar with.

Sorting Buttons

Collect different colors, sizes and shapes of buttons and put them into several small boxes. Set the boxes on a table. Have the children sit around the table. Give each child a Styrofoam food tray or other shallow container. Ask the children to decide what kinds of buttons they wish to sort out. For example, they could choose buttons that are red, buttons that have two holes or buttons that are square. Then have the children look for the appropriate buttons in the button boxes and place them in their trays.

Matching Buttons

Select twelve pairs of buttons. Glue one button from each pair to the bottom of an egg cup in an egg carton. Put the remaining buttons in a pile. Then have the children take turns placing the buttons from the pile into the cups that contain matching buttons.

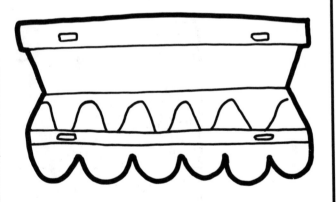

Our Button Song
Sung to: "Did You Ever See a Lassie?"

Let's sing a song of buttons,
Of buttons, of buttons.
Let's sing a song of buttons
That fasten our clothes.
There are big ones and small ones,
With two holes and four holes.
Let's sing a song of buttons
That fasten our clothes.

Alice Marks
Roseville, MN

Jenny Has Buttons
Sung to: "Mary Had a Little Lamb"

Jenny has buttons on her shirt,
On her shirt, on her shirt.
Jenny has buttons on her shirt,
Let's all count them now.
    (Count buttons.)

Substitute the names of your children for
"Jenny" and, when necessary, the names
of other articles of clothing for "shirt."

Alice Marks
Roseville, MN

Button Talk

Collect a handful of unusual buttons and give one to each child. Let the children take turns describing their buttons. If necessary, ask questions such as these: "What color is the button? How many holes does it have? What shape is it?"

Raisin Buttons

Give the children gingerbread people cookies, frosting, Popsicle sticks and raisins. Let the children spread the frosting on their cookies with the Popsicle sticks. Then have them add raisin "buttons" to their cookies before eating.

Children's Books:
- *Buttons*, Tom Robinson, (Penguin, 1976).
- *Corduroy*, Donald Freeman, (Viking, 1968).

Contributors:
Alice Marks, Roseville, MN

CAMERAS

Photo Frames

Take a photograph of each child. Cut frames out of posterboard to fit around the photos. Let the children decorate their frames with crayons, felt-tip markers, sequins, glitter or rickrack. Attach each child's picture to his or her frame and hang the photographs around the room.

Camera Observations

An old nonworking camera is a fun prop for young children. They seem to become more observant of things when pretending to take pictures. Let them pretend to take pictures of their friends and their surroundings and describe what they see through the camera lens.

My Very Own Camera

Sung to: ``The Oscar Meyer
    Theme Song''

Oh, I wish I had
My very own camera,
'Cause this is what
I'd really like to do.
I'd take some pictures of
My friends and family,
And then I'd give
A few of them to you.

Jean Warren

Picture Perfect

Hold up a pretend camera (or an old nonworking one). Tell the children that you want to take their pictures, but that they will have to follow your directions so that the pictures will be perfect. Have each child hold a block or other prop.

Then give directions such as these: ``Stand next to your block. Hold the block over your head. Put your hands around your block. Sit on your block. Put your block under your arm.''

Our Photo Album

Take photographs of places and people the children are familiar with (the local firehouse, a nearby park, the woman at the bakery down the street, etc.). Put the pictures in a photo album. Look at the pictures with the children and talk about the familiar places and faces.

Group Photos

Take photographs of the children involved in different activities. Later, use the pictures to stimulate a group discussion about the children and what they were doing.

Note: Make sure you have permission from parents before photographing the children.

Photo Books

At the beginning of the year, take a photograph of each child. Have the child place his or her photo on the bulletin board with a name card. At the end of the year, take another photo of each child and let the children make books about themselves. Have them place their earlier pictures at the beginnings of their books and their more recent pictures at the ends of their books. Let them fill the middle pages with drawings of their families, friends, pets, favorite foods, favorite activities, etc.

Children's Books:
- *Lights! Camera! Action!: How a Movie Is Made*, Gail Gibbons, (Harper, 1985).
- *Simple Pictures Are Best*, Nancy Willard, (Harcourt, 1977).

Contributors:
Betty Ruth Baker, Waco, TX

Cardboard Candles

Let the children paint empty toilet tissue tubes with tempera paint. When the tubes are dry, have the children glue them upright on small paper plates. Let the children decorate their candles and their plates with glitter, rickrack, pinecones and macaroni.

Variation: Let the children paint and decorate their candles. Then set the candles in bases of playdough and top with red, orange or yellow construction paper flames.

Candle Printing

Give the children various shapes and kinds of candles. Let them dip the candles into paint and use them to make prints on pieces of construction paper. Encourage the children to print with the bottoms and the sides of their candles.

Sounds Like "Wh"

Let the children carefully stand in front of one or more lighted candles. Encourage them to say words that begin with the "wh" sound ("where, why, who, when," etc.). Challenge them to blow out the candles by saying the "wh" sound correctly.

Caution: Activities that involve lighted candles require adult supervision at all times.

Eight Little Candles

Cut eight candle shapes and eight flame shapes out of felt. Arrange the candle shapes in a line on a flannelboard. Then read the poem below and let the children take turns placing the flames on the candles.

Eight little candles, one by one,
Were waiting to join the holiday fun.

The first little candle standing in the row,
Said, ''Light me now so I can glow.''

The second little candle, joining the plea,
Said, ''Light me, too, so I can see.''

The third little candle, wanting a turn,
Said, ''Light me now so I can burn.''

The fourth little candle standing in line,
Said, ''Light me, too, so I can shine.''

The fifth little candle, hoping for the same,
Said, ''I will dance if you light my flame.''

The sixth little candle, standing so straight,
Said, ''Light me now to celebrate.''

The seventh little candle, so happy tonight,
Said, ''It's my turn now to get a light.''

The eighth little candle, waiting so long,
Said, ''I may be last, but my light is strong.''

Now all eight candles are burning bright,
Filling the world with the wonder of light.

Jean Warren

Happy Candles

Sung to:"Twinkle, Twinkle, Little Star"

Happy candles burning bright,
Shining in the winter night.
Shining there for all to see,
Happy candles, one, two, three.
Happy candles burning bright,
Shine until the morning light.

Bonnie Woodard
Shreveport, LA

Candle Clock

Let the children watch time pass with a candle clock. Place two candles that are the same length in candle holders. Burn one candle for 30 minutes. Measure the difference in length between the two candles. Then use that measurement to mark lines down the side of the unburned candle. Set the first candle aside and light the marked candle while the children watch. Explain that when the candle burns down to the first line, 30 minutes will have gone by; when it burns down to the second line, another 30 minutes (or 60 minutes) will have gone by, etc. Then let the children periodically check the candle as it burns.

Caution: Activities that involve lighted candles require adult supervision at all times.

Counting Candles

Have the children pretend that it's someone's birthday and let them make cakes out of playdough. Set the cakes on small plates, jar lids or in small pans. Have the children decorate their cakes with straw sections to represent birthday candles. As they place the candles on their cakes, have them count the candles.

Measuring Candles

Collect many different sizes of candles. Set out the candles and let the children take turns lining them up from smallest to largest.

Candle Salads

To make each salad place a pineapple ring on top of a lettuce leaf. Stand half of a peeled banana upright in the center of the pineapple ring. Cut off the pointed end of the banana. Use a vegetable peeler to peel off a strip of carrot. Roll the carrot strip into a ring, overlapping the ends. Stick one end of a toothpick through the ends of the carrot strip and one end down into the banana. Pinch the carrot ring to make it look like a pointed candle flame.

Children's Books:
- *Candle for Christmas*, Jean Speare, (Macmillan, 1987).
- *Ox-Cart Man*, Donald Hall, (Viking, 1979).

Contributors:
Sophia Drake, Jamaica, NY
Sr. Linda Kaman, R.S.M., Pittsburgh, PA

CANS

Decorative Cans

Collect empty cans, wash them
and smooth over any rough edges.
Let the children decorate the cans
with colorful self-stick paper or by
gluing on wallpaper, felt, fabric,
shells or magazine cutouts. Then
let them use their decorated cans
as holders for straws, buttons,
puzzle pieces, games or crayons.

Hint: If desired, let the children
give their decorated cans as gifts.

Printing With Cans

Glue pieces of yarn in various
patterns on the sides of empty
cans. Place folded paper towels in
shallow containers and pour small
amounts of tempera paint on top.

Have the children roll the cans
across the paint pads, then roll
them on pieces of construction
paper to make prints.

Planters

Let the children plant seeds or rooted cuttings in attractively decorated cans. (Punch holes in the bottoms of the cans for drainage.) Have the children water their plants as needed and check them weekly for signs of growth.

Water Fun

Place a number of cans on the water table and let the children experiment with filling, pouring and measuring. Later, use objects such as nails or a hand can opener to punch holes in the covered ends of the cans. Vary the number, kinds and sizes of the holes. Different sizes of cans and holes will encourage the children to observe, discuss and explore.

Sizing Up Cans

Collect a variety of cans from small to large. Let the children take turns arranging the cans in order by size.

Circle Cans

On a piece of posterboard, trace around the bottoms of various-sized cans. Cut out the circles you have traced. Give the children the circles and the cans. Let them take turns matching the circles to the appropriate cans.

Grocery Shopping

Set out a small grocery basket and cans with labels attached. Ask the children to fill the basket with cans that have similar kinds of foods pictured on the labels, such as fruits, vegetables or soups.

Listening Practice

To increase the auditory skills of the children, choose three or four cans of various sizes. Have the children close their eyes and listen carefully as you tap the cans with your hand, a ruler or an eraser. Let the children repeat your sound patterns on cans of their own.

Musical Instruments

Let the children decorate cans that have plastic lids with construction paper, rickrack, felt or stickers. Let them make drums out of their decorated cans by putting on the plastic lids. Or have them make maracas by placing handfuls of pebbles, rice, seeds or foam pieces in the cans and covering both ends with plastic lids. Let the children make their own music by beating their drums and shaking their maracas.

Fruit Bread Rounds

Heat ½ cup raisins in ¼ cup unsweetened frozen apple juice concentrate until the raisins are tender (approximately 3 minutes). Place raisins in a blender and puree. Then add 1 sliced banana, ½ cup vegetable oil, 1 teaspoon vanilla, ½ cup canned pumpkin and 1 egg and blend again. In a large bowl mix or sift together 1 cup whole-wheat flour, ¼ cup wheat germ, ½ teaspoon baking powder, ½ teaspoon baking soda, ¼ teaspoon salt and 1 tablespoon cinnamon. Pour in pumpkin mixture and stir well. Remove the labels from 2 empty 16-ounce vegetable cans. Wash and dry the cans and spray the insides with nonstick vegetable cooking spray. Fill cans approximately ¾ full with the bread mixture. Place in oven and bake at 350 degrees for 50 to 60 minutes. Let cool. Remove bread from cans and slice into ¼-inch rounds. Serve plain or spread with cream cheese that has been mixed with a small amount of unsweetened frozen apple juice concentrate. Makes 16 servings.

Children's Books:
- *Gregory, the Terrible Eater,* Mitchell Sharmat, (Macmillan, 1980).

Contributors:
Rose C. Merenda, Warwick, RI

Egg Carton Caterpillars

Cut off the tops of cardboard egg cartons and save them for other uses. Then cut the bottom sections of the egg cartons in half lengthwise. Turn the sections over and have the children paint them green, brown or orange (or whatever color they desire) to make caterpillar bodies. Help them poke pipe cleaners into the tops of their caterpillar heads to make antennae. Then have the children draw eyes and mouths on their caterpillars with felt-tip markers.

Pattern Caterpillars

Cut a large number of 1-inch circles from black and orange construction paper. Have the children create caterpillars by gluing the circles together, alternating colors to form patterns. Let them add circle stickers for eyes and construction paper antennae, if desired.

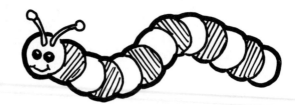

Caterpillar Life Cycle

Discuss the life cycle of a caterpillar with the children. Explain that caterpillars go through four distinct life stages – the egg, the larva (caterpillar), the pupa (chrysalis or cocoon) and the adult (butterfly or moth). Make sequence cards with pictures of the four stages on them. Let the children take turns putting them in order.

Hungry Caterpillars

Read the poem below. Then ask the children what they would eat if they were hungry caterpillars.

What do caterpillars do?
Nothing but chew and chew.
What do caterpillars know?
Nothing much but how to grow.

They just eat what by and by
Will make them be a butterfly.
But this is more than I can do
However much I chew and chew!

Author Unknown

Caterpillar Crawl

Have the children form a "caterpillar" by lining up in a row on their knees. Ask each child to hold onto the back or the legs of the person in front of him or her.

Then have the children crawl together in a line by taking steps first with their right knees, then with their left knees.

Sleeping Caterpillars

Bring in a sleeping bag to use as a chrysalis and place it on the floor. Let one child at a time pretend to be a caterpillar and crawl inside the sleeping bag. Then have

everyone sing the first verse of the song below. When the child crawls out of the sleeping bag, have everyone sing the second verse.

Sung to: "Goodnight Ladies"

Goodnight, caterpillar,
Goodnight, caterpillar.
Goodnight, caterpillar,
You'll be a butterfly.

Merrily you fly away,
Fly away, fly away.
Merrily you fly away,
Pretty butterfly.

Barbara Vilet
Naperville, IL

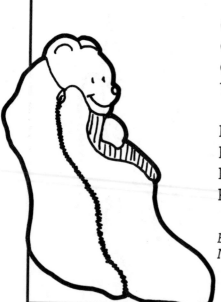

Crawling All Around

Sung to: "Frere Jacques"

Caterpillar, caterpillar,
Crawl, crawl, crawl;
Crawl, crawl, crawl.
Crawling on the ground,
Crawling all around.
Crawl, crawl, crawl;
Crawl, crawl, crawl.

Jean Warren

The Fuzzy Caterpillar

Sung to: "Eensy, Weensy Spider"

The fuzzy caterpillar
Curled up on a leaf,
Spun her little chrysalis
And then fell fast asleep.
While she was sleeping,
She dreamed that she could fly,
And later when she woke up
She was a butterfly!

Elizabeth McKinnon

Melon Ball Caterpillars

To make each caterpillar, fasten three melon balls together with toothpicks. In one of the end melon balls, partially insert two whole cloves for antennae. Serve each melon ball caterpillar on a lettuce leaf.

Note: Have the children remove the cloves and the toothpicks before eating their melon ball caterpillars.

Children's Books:
- *Caterpillar and the Polliwog*, Jack Kent, (Prentice Hall, 1982).
- *If at First You Do Not See*, Ruth Brown, (Henry Holt, 1983).
- *The Very Hungry Caterpillar*, Eric Carle, (Putnam, 1981).

Contributors:
Paula Schneider, Kent, WA
Jane M. Spannbauer, South St. Paul, MN
Barbara Vilet, Naperville, IL

Kitty Collage

Cover a bulletin board or a wall with a large sheet of butcher paper. Let the children search through old magazines for pictures of cats. Have them tear or cut out the pictures and paste them on the butcher paper. Then lead the children in a discussion about cats. Have them compare the colors and sizes of the cats in the pictures and talk about what the cats are doing.

The Three Little Kittens

Read the nursery rhyme "The Three Little Kittens" with the children. Cut three kitten shapes out of felt. Then cut three pairs of mitten shapes out of three different colors of felt. Place the kitten shapes on a flannelboard. Mix up the six mitten shapes and place them below the kittens. Have the children help the kittens find their lost mittens by placing a matching colored pair on each kitten.

Variation: Instead of matching colored mittens, have the children match mittens of different shapes, sizes or patterns.

Color Cats

Cut cat shapes out of red, blue, yellow, brown, green, black and white construction paper. Let the children decorate the cat shapes with crayons or felt-tip markers. Attach Popsicle sticks to the backs of the shapes to make puppets. Have the children sit in a circle.

Ask them to name the colors of their cat puppets. Then read the poem below. As the children hear the names of colors that are the same as the colors of their cats, have them raise their cat puppets and say "Mee-ow."

When the cat that is red
Is finally fed,
He raises his head
And says — "Mee-ow!"

When the cat that is blue
Has nothing to do,
He comes up, too,
And whispers — "Mee-ow!"

When the cat that is yellow
Is feeling mellow,
He tends to stretch
And bellow — "Mee-ow!"

When the cat that is brown
Starts stalking the town,
You'll hear his sound
When he cries — "Mee-ow!"

When the cat that is green
Is finally seen,
You'll know what I mean
When I say he can really —
   "Mee-ow!"

When the cat that is black
Arches his back,
He has an uncanny knack
Of screeching — "Mee-ow!"

When the cat that is white
Comes into your sight,
You very well might
Hear his famous — "Mee-ow!"

Okay, little cats,
Let's hear some "Mee-ows!"
And now it's time
For curtsies and bows.

Susan M. Paprocki
Northbrook, IL

My Kitten
Sung to: "Sing a Song of Sixpence"

I have a little kitten,
She's black and white and gray.
When I try to cuddle her,
She always wants to play.
So I drag a piece of yarn
Across the kitchen floor.
She thinks it is a little mouse
To chase right out the door.

Elizabeth Vollrath
Stevens Point, WI

I'm a Little Kitten
Sung to: "I'm a Little Teapot"

I'm a little kitten,
Soft and furry.
I'll be your friend,
So don't you worry.
Right up on your lap I like to hop,
Purr, purr, purr, and never stop.

Betty Silkunas
Lansdale, PA

Cat Puzzles

Cut large cat shapes out of poster-board. Cover the shapes with clear self-stick paper and cut each one into several large interlocking puzzle pieces. This activity is perfect for small fingers. For older children, increase the difficulty by cutting each puzzle into smaller pieces.

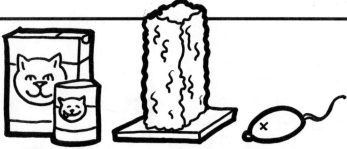

Cat Care

Invite a cat expert such as a veterinarian, a pet shop owner or an animal shelter employee to bring in a cat or a kitten to show to your group. Ask the cat expert to demonstrate the proper way to hold a cat and to discuss such topics as feeding, grooming techniques and exercise. If possible, arrange to have him or her bring in samples of cat supplies such as a feeding dish, a scratching post and a rubber mouse or catnip toy.

Listening Game

Have the children sit in a circle. Choose one child to be the mother or father cat and to sit in the middle of the circle. While the cat hides his or her eyes, pick several children to be baby kittens by tapping their shoulders. Have the baby kittens quickly find hiding spots in the room and make soft mewing sounds. Then have the mother or father cat search for the kittens, listening carefully for their mewing sounds as clues to their locations.

Children's Books:
- *Do Not Open*, Brinton Turkle, (Dutton, 1981).
- *Have You Seen My Cat?*, Eric Carle, (Picture Book Studio, 1987).
- *Millions of Cats*, Wanda Gag, (Putnam, 1977).

Contributors:
Susan M. Paprocki, Northbrook, IL

Circle Caterpillars

For each child cut six circles out of colored construction paper. Let the children overlap and glue their circles in straight lines on pieces of white construction paper. Then let them draw antennae, legs and faces on their lines of circles to make caterpillars.

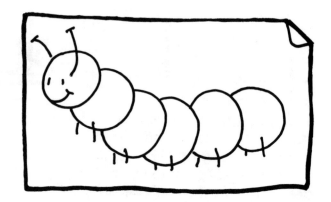

Circle Trees

Draw a tree with bare branches on a large piece of blue paper and attach fringed green construction paper below it for grass. Let the children glue circles they have punched out of construction paper with a hole punch on the branches and beneath the tree. Carefully shake off the extra circles. To make an autumn scene have the children punch out red, yellow and orange circles; to make a winter scene, white circles; to make a spring scene, pink circles; to make a summer scene, green circles.

Number Cards

Draw or glue from one to ten circles on the top halves of ten index cards. Write the corresponding number under each set of circles on the lower parts of the cards and cut them in half. Let the children take turns matching the circles with the corresponding numbers.

Circle Patterns

For each child put three or four different colored self-stick circles in a row to make a pattern on a piece of paper. Then give the children more colored circles and let them continue the patterns on their papers.

Variation: Instead of self-stick circles, use circles that have been punched out of colored construction paper with a hole punch.

Size Circles

Cut eight different sized circles out of the same color of posterboard. Mix them up and have the children arrange the circles by size.

My Favorite Shape Is a Circle
Sung to: "My Bonnie Lies Over the Ocean"

My favorite shape is a circle,
Because it's as round as can be.
The world is just full of these circles,
So think hard and name one for me.
Snowman, snowman,
The snowman's a circle or two or three.
Snowman, snowman,
The snowman's a circle you see.

My favorite shape is a circle,
Because it's as round as can be.
The world is just full of these circles,
So think hard and name one for me.
Pizza, pizza,
The pizza's a circle you eat.
Pizza, pizza,
The pizza's a circle you eat.

Continue with similar verses, letting the children name other things that are shaped like circles.

Barbara Dunn
Hollidaysburg, PA

Vegetable Rounds
Slice carrots, cucumbers and zucchini into rounds. Let the children spread them with cream cheese, peanut butter or egg salad for snacktime.

Pizzas
Toast English muffins and let the children spoon on tomato sauce and grated cheese before adding round pepperoni and olive slices to make pizzas. Bake at 350 degrees until the cheese is melted.

Musical Circles

Cut circles out of colored construction paper or posterboard and tape them to the floor. Have the children march around the circles as you play music. When you stop the music, have the children find circles to stand on. Ask them to identify the colors of their circles before playing the music again.

Hula-Hoop Games

Bring in a Hula-Hoop and place it in the center of the floor. Have the children take turns walking around the outside of the hoop, heel to toe, without touching it. Then let them try jumping in and out of the Hula-Hoop, walking around it with one foot inside and one foot outside, etc. If desired, demonstrate how to use the Hula-Hoop and let the children try using it, too.

Children's Books:
- *Circles, Triangles and Squares,* Tana Hoban, (Macmillan, 1974).
- *Look Around! A Book About Shapes,* Leonard Fisher, (Viking, 1987).
- *Shapes,* John Reiss, (Macmillan, 1987).

Contributors:
Barbara Dunn, Hollidaysburg, PA
Deborah A. Roessel, Flemington, NJ

CLOWNS

Creating Clowns

Cut circles, squares, rectangles, triangles and other geometric shapes out of construction paper in a variety of sizes and colors. Let the children glue the shapes on pieces of construction paper to create clown faces.

Four Little Clowns

Make four felt clowns that match the descriptions of the characters in the poem below. As you read the poem, let the children take turns placing the appropriate clowns on a flannelboard.

This little clown is jolly and fat.
This little clown wears a big red hat.
This little clown is strong and tall.
This little clown is wee and small,
But he does the funniest tricks of all!

Paula C. Foreman
Millersville, PA

Carl the Clown

Cut a clown face out of white felt and use felt scraps or felt-tip markers to make hair and facial features. Then cut one clown hat shape from each of the following colors of felt: red, yellow, blue, purple, white, green and brown. Place the clown face on a flannelboard. As you recite the poem below, put the appropriate colored hats on the clown's head. When the children have become familiar with the poem, let them take turns placing the hats on the clown's head themselves.

My name, boys and girls, is Carl the Clown.
I wear my hats all over town.

Each one has its own color name,
Which you can learn if you play my game.

Oh, here's a hat, and it is red.
It fits so nicely on my head.

Now when I wear my hat of yellow,
I'm told I'm quite a dandy fellow.

I hope you like my hat of blue.
I'll put it on now, just for you.

My purple hat is just for good.
I'd wear it always if I could.

I wear a white hat on a sunny day.
It looks quite nice, my friends all say.

I put on my green hat to visit the park,
But I take it off when it gets dark.

And when it's dark, I put on brown.
This hat is for a sleepy clown.

Susan M. Paprocki
Northbrook, IL

Matching Clowns

Make five felt clown faces with collars attached. Number the clowns from 1 to 5 by gluing the appropriate number of felt dots on the collars. Then make five felt clown hats and number them from 1 to 5 by gluing on felt numerals. Let the children place the clown faces on a flannelboard. Then have them match the numerals on the hats with the dots on the collars and put the hats on the clowns' heads.

Variation: Cut hat and collar shapes out of different colors or textures of fabric and let the children match them accordingly.

Did You Ever See a Clown?

Have the children form a circle. Choose one child to be the clown and stand in the middle. As everyone sings the song below, have the clown act out funny movements for the other children to imitate. Continue until every child has had a turn being the clown.

Sung to: "Did You Ever See a Lassie?"

Did you ever see a clown,
A clown, a clown?
Did you ever see a clown
Move this way and that?
Move this way and that way,
Move this way and that way.
Did you ever see a clown
Move this way and that?

Paula C. Foreman
Millersville, PA

Clown Parade

Play circus music and let the children pretend to be clowns as they march around the room. Encourage them to move in funny ways like clowns would.

We Are Clowns Today
Sung to: "The Farmer in the Dell"

We are clowns today,
We are clowns today.
Heigh-ho the derry-oh,
We are clowns today.

We do tricks today,
We do tricks today.
Heigh-ho the derry-oh,
We do tricks today.

Let the children make up other verses and act out the movements as they sing.

Paula C. Foreman
Millersville, PA

Funny Clowns
Sung to: "Frere Jacques"

Funny clowns, funny clowns,
Jump around, jump around.
Sometimes making faces,
Sometimes running races.
Funny clowns, funny clowns.

Funny clowns, funny clowns,
Spin around, spin around.
Sometimes with big noses,
Sometimes with big toes-es,
Funny clowns, funny clowns.

Jean Warren

Clown Face Salads

For each child place a scoop of cottage cheese on a small plate. Make clown faces by adding cherry tomato noses, green pepper ears, olive eyes, red pepper mouths and lettuce bow ties.

Variation: Instead of vegetables, use a variety of fruits to create the clown faces.

Children's Books:
• *Clown-Arounds Go on Vacation,* Joanna Cole, (Parents, 1984).
• *Sing, Pierrot, Sing: A Picture Book in Mime,* Tomie De Paola, (Harcourt, 1983).

Contributors:
Paula C. Foreman, Millersville, PA

Cookie Cutter Art

Trace around cookie cutters on Styrofoam food trays and cut out the shapes. Have the children place the Styrofoam shapes on different colors of construction paper. Let them dip toothbrushes in paint and rub tongue depressors across the toothbrushes, spattering paint onto their papers. Then let them remove the shapes to reveal the pictures they have created.

Cookie Cutter Printing

Pour tempera paint on folded paper towels placed in several Styrofoam food trays. Let the children dip cookie cutters into the paint and press them on pieces of construction paper to make prints.

Five Little Cookies

Cut five cookie shapes out of felt, one each from white, green, yellow, brown and red. Place the cookie shapes on a flannelboard. As you recite the poem below, let the children take turns removing the appropriate colored cookies.

Variation: Use Christmas cookie shapes and change the first line of the poem to "Five little Christmas cookies."

Five little cookies,
With frosting galore.
Mother ate the white one,
And then there were four.

Four little cookies,
Two and two, you see.
Father ate the green one,
And then there were three.

Three little cookies,
But before I knew,
Sister ate the yellow one,
And then there were two.

Two little cookies,
Oh, what fun.
Brother ate the brown one,
And then there was one.

One little cookie,
Watch me run.
I ate the red one,
And then there were none.

Adapted Traditional

Cookie Match-Ups

On a heavy piece of paper trace around three or four cookie cutters with a felt-tip marker. Then mix up the cookie cutters and let the children place them on the appropriate shapes for a simple matching game.

Cookie Cutter Puzzles

Place cookie cutters on Styrofoam food trays and press down hard to make indentations. Use a sharp knife to carefully cut out the shapes. Let the children put the puzzles together by placing the cookie shapes in the appropriate cut-out spaces in the trays.

Variation: Instead of Styrofoam food trays, use sturdy box lids.

Sandwich Shapes

Let the children help make egg salad, peanut butter and jelly or cheese sandwiches. Then have them use cookie cutters to cut shapes out of their sandwiches.

Sandwich Decorations

Let the children help make open-faced sandwiches by spreading soft cream cheese on slices of whole-wheat bread. Have the children place open cookie cutters on top of their sandwiches and fill them with alfalfa sprouts. Then let the children remove their cookie cutters to reveal their sandwich decorations.

Children's Books:
• *If You Give a Mouse a Cookie*, Laura Numeroff, (Harper, 1985).

Contributors:
Barbara Robinson, Glendale, AZ
Beth Weissman, Dayton, OH

Corn Collages

Cut corncob shapes out of yellow construction paper and corn husk shapes out of green construction paper. Let the children glue the husks on the sides of their corncobs. Then have them brush glue over the cob sections and press on dried corn or popcorn kernels. Some children will be content to just sprinkle on the kernels at random, while others will meticulously arrange them in rows.

Corncob Prints

Wash corncobs and let them dry for several days. Make paint pads by placing folded paper towels in shallow containers and pouring on liquid tempera paint. Let the children roll the corncobs on the paint pads, then roll the cobs across sheets of construction paper to make prints.

Time for Corn

Read the following poem and let
the children act out the
movements.

Great big giant cornstalk,
Growing in the sun.
Ripe juicy ears of corn –
Let's pick some.

Juicy tender yellow corn,
Put it in the pot.
Pour in the water –
Cook it till it's hot.

Juicy tender sweet corn,
Ready on the plate.
Is it time for dinner?
I can't wait!

Jean Warren

Comparing Corn Items

Set out a variety of corn items for
the children to touch and
compare. For example, you might
include cornstalks, ears of fresh
corn, dried Indian corn, popcorn
kernels, popped popcorn, canned
corn, cornmeal, cornflakes and
corn chips.

Sprouting Corn

Place dirt in a small Ziploc bag.
Add water and a few kernels of
popcorn. Seal the bag and hang it
in a sunny window. The popcorn
kernels will begin to sprout in
about a week.

Estimating Kernels

Place some popcorn kernels in a small clear plastic container and let the children estimate how many kernels it contains. After everyone has had a turn estimating, pour out the kernels and count them together.

Cornmeal Measuring

Let the children take turns playing in a dishpan of cornmeal. Provide a set of measuring cups. Help the children discover that it takes four quarter-cups or two half-cups to equal one cup.

Extension: Add small sand toys to the dishpan for the children to play with.

Standing in the Corn Field
Sung to: ``Skip to My Lou''

Standing in the corn field out in the sun,
Picking some big ears one by one,
Cooking up the yellow corn, boy, what fun.
Munching on sweet corn. Yum, yum, yum!

Jean Warren

Corn on the Cob

Let the children help you shuck some fresh corn. Boil the corn and cut it into small sections. Allow the corn to cool before serving it at snacktime.

Corn Chowder

Let the children help you prepare your favorite corn chowder recipe for lunch or snacktime.

Corn Chips

Combine ½ cup yellow cornmeal and ½ teaspoon salt in a mixing bowl. Pour in 1 cup boiling water and stir. Add 1 teaspoon margarine and stir until melted. Add another ¾ cup boiling water and continue stirring. Drop small spoonfuls of the mixture (about the size of a half-dollar) on a greased cookie sheet. Then bake at 425 degrees for 12 to 15 minutes or until lightly browned. Makes approximately 3 dozen chips.

Children's Books:
- *Corn Is Maize: The Gift of the Indians*, Aliki, (Harper, 1976).

Contributors:
Neoma Kreuter, Ontario, CA
Joyce Warden, Philadelphia, PA

Rope Frames

Give each child a 10- by 12-inch piece of cardboard and 4 feet of thin rope or twine. Have the children glue their rope pieces around the edges of their cardboard sheets to make rope frames. Then let them glue pieces of their own artwork or pictures cut from magazines inside their frames.

Variation: Take photos of the children dressed up as cowboys or cowgirls and let them glue their photos inside their frames to give as gifts.

Riding on the Range

Have the children sit in a circle. Let them take turns slapping their thighs (to sound like horses galloping) and saying, "When I go out riding on the range, I always take my _____." Have each child repeat the items mentioned by the previous players and add a new one of his or her own.

Hint: If the children are too young to remember a long list of items, start the list over frequently or just let each child tell what he or she would take on such a journey.

Cowboy Clothes

Cut the following shapes out of felt: a cowboy or cowgirl figure, a hat, a bandanna, a jacket, pants, boots and a vest. Place the figure on a flannelboard and let the children take turns dressing the cowboy or cowgirl, naming each article of clothing as they put it on.

Cowboy Hat Matching

Cut twelve cowboy hat shapes out of construction paper. Divide the hats into pairs. Color the bands on each pair differently, using stripes, dots or patterns. Mix up the shapes and let the children take turns finding the pairs of hats that have matching bands.

Dress-Up Fun

Have the children dress up in Western gear and pretend to be cowboys or cowgirls out on the range. Let them act out the various ways that cowboys and cowgirls used their hats, bandannas and ropes. If authentic items are unavailable, let the children use wide-brimmed straw or felt hats as Western hats, squares of colored cloth as bandannas and pieces of clothesline or other thin rope as lariats.

I've Been Riding on the Range

Sung to: "I've been Working on the
   Railroad"

I've been riding on the range,
All the livelong day.
I've been riding on the range,
Herding dogies on their way.
Can't you hear the cowboys shouting,
"Yippity-oh-ky-yay!"
Can't you hear the cowboys shouting,
"Dogies, move this way!"

Repeat, substituting "cowgirls" for
"cowboys." Explain to the children that
"dogies" are stray or motherless calves.

Jean Warren

Move On, Little Dogies

Sung to: "My Bonnie Lies Over
   the Ocean"

All day I ride on the prairie,
All night I sleep on the ground.
Oh, I'm a roaming cowboy,
Who travels around and around.
Move on, move on,
Move on, little dogies, move on,
   move on.
Move on, move on,
Move on, little dogies, move on.

Repeat, substituting "cowgirl" for
"cowboy."

Jean Warren

Chuck Wagon

When cowboys worked on the range, they were followed by the chuck wagon which the cook (called a ``cookie'') used as a kitchen to prepare such foods as beans, bacon, beef jerky, biscuits and dried fruits. Make a ``chuck wagon'' by bending and taping a large piece of posterboard over the top of an ordinary wagon. Choose someone to be the ``cookie'' and let him or her deliver the day's snack in the chuck wagon.

Beef Jerky

Cover 1 to 2 pounds flank steak (sliced into ¼-inch strips) with marinade sauce (¼ cup soy sauce, ¼ cup Worcestershire sauce, pepper, salt, onion salt, garlic powder to taste) and refrigerate for 6 to 8 hours. Stir occasionally. Drain and place strips on a rack over a shallow pan (or use a broiler pan). Bake at 150 degrees for 8 to 10 hours until dried. Cool and eat or store in a tightly covered container. If the jerky is to be eaten right away, 8 hours of drying time should be sufficient and will make chewing easier for young children.

Children's Books:
- *Barn Dance,* Bill Martin, (Henry Holt, 1986).
- *Ridin' That Strawberry Roan,* Marcia Sewall, (Viking, 1985).
- *White Dynamite and Curly Kid,* Bill Martin, (Henry Holt, 1986).

DINOSAURS

Dinosaur Facts

Lead the children in a discussion about dinosaurs. Depending on the ages and abilities of the children, discuss some or all of the following concepts.

Dinosaurs are thought to have been reptiles. Begin by introducing and discussing the characteristics of modern-day reptiles such as turtles, snakes and lizards.

Dinosaurs lived long ago. Try to give the children an idea of how long ago they lived by contrasting the world the children know and the world in which dinosaurs existed. Were there any people, houses or cars? Where did dinosaurs live? What did the world look like? What did dinosaurs like to do? If desired, have the children draw pictures depicting a world with dinosaurs.

Dinosaurs are extinct. Ask the children to talk about why they think dinosaurs disappeared. (Accept all answers.) Then mention two of the main theories scientists have for their disappearance: the climate became too cold and most plant and animal life died, possibly as a result of the continental drift altering ocean currents and wind patterns; or a meteorite or comet hit the earth and filled the atmosphere with so much dust that light from the sun could not reach the earth, causing plants, then animals to die.

We learn about dinosaurs by studying fossils. Explain that fossils are "evidence of plant and animal life usually preserved in rocks." Talk about how scientists learn more about dinosaurs by carefully digging up fossils and studying them. Ask the children why scientists can't talk to people who have seen dinosaurs or taken pictures of them.

There were many different kinds of dinosaurs (large and small, plant-eaters and meat-eaters, dinosaurs who lived on the land and dinosaurs who lived in the water).

More Dinosaur Facts

Help the children learn about individual dinosaurs. Illustrations and information about five well-known dinosaurs follow.

Apatosaurus (''deceptive reptile''): This dinosaur used to be called ''Brontosaurus.'' It weighed about 30 tons and stood 15 feet tall at the shoulder. Its long neck allowed it to feed on the vegetation that was up high.

Stegosaurus (''roofed reptile''): The Stegosaurus had large bony plates along its back and a spiked tail. It was 20 feet long and weighed 3,000 pounds or more. It was a plant-eater.

Triceratops (''three-horned face''): The Triceratops had three horns, one on its nose and one over each eye. It also had a shield of bone, called a ''frill,'' around its head. It was a plant-eater.

Tyrannosaurus (''tyrant reptile''): The Tyrannosaurus was the largest meat-eater, weighing up to 7 tons. It measured as much as 46 feet from the tip of its nose to the end of its tail. It had 60 very sharp teeth.

Pteranodon (''winged and toothless''): The Pteranodon was one of the largest flying reptiles. Its diet primarily consisted of ocean fish. Its wings were made of leathery skin stretched across a single finger.

Dinosaur Crowns

Cut sponges into the shapes of Tyrannosaurus dinosaur footprints. Fold paper towels in half and place them in shallow containers. Pour a small amount of brown tempera paint on top of each towel. Give the children crowns cut out of construction paper. Let the children cover their crowns with dinosaur footprints by pressing the sponge stamps first into the paint and then onto their papers. When the paint has dried, write "Tyrannosaurus <u>(child's name)</u>" on the front of each crown.

Stuffed Dinosaurs

For each child cut two dinosaur shapes out of brown paper bags or brown butcher paper. Have the children hold their shapes together while you staple around three sides. Then let them crumple small pieces of newspaper and stuff them into their dinosaur shapes. When the shapes are full, staple the remaining sides closed. Let the children decorate their stuffed dinosaurs with paint. When the dinosaur shapes are dry, attach loops of yarn to them and hang them around the room.

Variation: Punch holes around the edges of the pairs of dinosaur shapes and let children lace them together with yarn.

Fossil Hunt

Bury several plastic dinosaurs in a large pan of cornmeal and place the pan on a table. Let the children take turns going on a "fossil hunt." Give the children spoons to use to dig in the cornmeal. When a dinosaur "fossil" is discovered, ask the children to identify it by looking carefully at its characteristics.

Variation: This activity can also be done in a sandbox.

Playdough Fossils

Make gray playdough by adding a small amount of powdered black tempera paint to your regular recipe. Set the playdough and some plastic dinosaurs on a table. Let the children make "fossils" by pressing the dinosaurs into the playdough and then carefully removing them to see the imprints left behind.

Alphabet Puzzles

Cut 26 identical dinosaur shapes from posterboard. Use a felt-tip marker to print upper-case letters at the tops of the shapes and corresponding lower-case letters at the bottoms. Cut each dinosaur shape into two puzzle pieces. Give the children the pieces and let them take turns putting the puzzles together by matching the upper- and lower-case letters.

Dinosaur Fact Book

Have the children take turns dictating a favorite dinosaur fact to you. Write each child's fact on a separate sheet of paper and let him or her illustrate the fact with crayons, felt-tip markers or dinosaur stickers or stamps. Staple the pages together to make a Dinosaur Fact Book.

Tyrannosaurus Toss

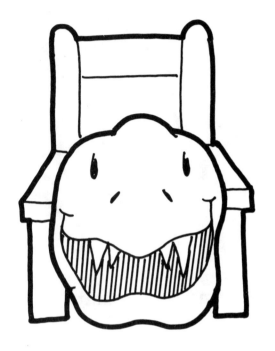

Draw a picture of a large Tyrannosaurus head on a piece of sturdy cardboard. Use a sharp knife to cut out the dinosaur's mouth, including lots of teeth. Then prop the cardboard Tyrannosaurus head against a chair or secure it with tape across a doorway. Give the children bean bags and let them take turns "feeding the dinosaur" by tossing the bean bags into its mouth.

Prehistoric Parade

Play different types of instrumental music. Have the children move around the room, pretending to be the dinosaurs that the music reminds them of. For example, a march might remind them of Tyrannosauruses; light airy music, Pteranodons; slow music, Apatosauruses, munching on plants in a swamp. When you stop the music, encourage the children to tell you which dinosaurs they were.

DINOSAURS

Tyrannosaurus Rex
Sung to: "Mary Had a Little Lamb"

Dinosaurs walked on this earth,
On this earth, on this earth.
Dinosaurs walked on this earth,
A long, long time ago.

Tyrannosaurus Rex was the king,
Was the king, was the king.
Tyrannosaurus Rex was the king,
A long, long time ago.

Tyrannosaurus (child's name) was the king,
Was the king, was the king.
Tyrannosaurus (child's name) was the king,
A long, long time ago.

Let the children wear their crowns from the activity on page 108 while singing the song.

Rosemary Giordano
Philadelphia, PA

All Around the Swamp
Sung to: "The Wheels on the Bus"

The Pteranodon's wings went
Flap, flap, flap,
Flap, flap, flap,
Flap, flap, flap.
The Pteranodon's wings went
Flap, flap, flap,
All around the swamp.

Additional verses: "The Tyrannosaurus Rex went grr, grr, grr; The Triceratops' horns went poke, poke, poke; The Apatosaurus went munch, munch, munch; The Stegosaurus' tail went spike, spike, spike."

Yosie Yoshimura
Gardena, CA

Dinosaurs

Sung to: "Oh, My Darling Clementine"

Great big dinosaurs, great big dinosaurs,
Lived so long ago.
Some liked land and some liked water,
Some flew in the air.

Great big dinosaurs, great big dinosaurs,
Lived so long ago.
Some had horns and some had spikes,
Some had wings like bats.

Great big dinosaurs, great big dinosaurs,
Lived so long ago.
Some ate plants and some ate meat,
But now there are no more.

Allane Eastberg, Jennifer Eastberg
Gig Harbor, WA

Dinosaur Delights

Give each child two pieces of hot dog, two broccoli florets and a small amount of salad dressing for dipping. Talk about the meat-eating dinosaurs as the children devour their hot dog pieces and the plant-eaters as they munch their broccoli. Point out that meat-eaters had lots of sharp teeth while plant-eaters had square, flat teeth.

Children's Books:
- *Danny and the Dinosaur*, Syd Hoff, (Harper Row, 1978).
- *Patrick's Dinosaurs*, Carol Carrick, (Houghton Mifflin, 1983).
- *Prehistoric Pinkerton*, Steven Kellogg, (Dial, 1987).

Contributors:
Rosemary Giordano, Philadelphia, PA
Leigh McCune, Tucson, AZ
Nancy C. Windes, Denver, CO

Eggshell Collages

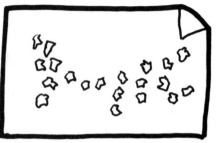

Save the shells from a number of eggs and dye them with food coloring. Set out small containers of the dyed eggshells and liquid glue. Give each child a Q-Tip or a small brush and a piece of construction paper. Have the children paint designs or pictures on their papers with the glue. Then have them sprinkle the dyed eggshells on their papers and shake off the excess.

Hint: To dye eggshells, add 1 teaspoon vinegar and a few drops of food coloring to ½ cup hot water. Drop crushed eggshells into the dye. Stir and spoon them out when the shells are the desired color. Allow the shells to dry in a warm (200 degrees) oven on a cookie sheet.

Variation: Have the children glue plain white eggshells on pieces of colored construction paper.

Happy Eggs, Sad Eggs

For each child cut two large egg shapes out of construction paper. Draw a happy face on one egg shape and a sad face on the other. Give a pair of the egg shapes to each child. Then have the children hold up their happy or sad egg faces in response to such statements as these: "I played with a friend today; I fell and hurt myself; It's my birthday today." Let the children take turns making their own statements for the others to respond to with their happy or sad egg faces.

Memory Eggs

Place two or three different colored eggs in an empty egg carton. Show the eggs to the children and then close the lid. Ask the children to name the colors they remember seeing. Open the lid to show the children the actual eggs. Continue the game, adding a different colored egg each time.

Color Cups

To make this game, you will need an empty egg carton and several different colored eggs. Mark the bottom of each egg cup with a color corresponding to one of the eggs. Then let the children take turns placing the eggs in the matching colored cups.

Hint: For the games on this page, purchase plastic eggs from a craft store; have the children paint Styrofoam eggs a variety of colors; or paint blown eggs with tempera, then shellac.

Pattern Eggs

Draw and cut out six large cardboard eggs. Glue a different pattern of fabric or wallpaper to each egg. Cut the eggs in half. Let the children take turns matching the egg halves.

Pass the Egg

Have the children sit in a circle. Let them pass around a hard-boiled egg while you play or sing a favorite tune. When you stop the music, the child holding the egg becomes the "egg-ceptional player."

Egg Relay

As a fun part of your "eggs-traordinary unit," plan an old-fashioned egg relay. Let the children roll eggs across the floor using straws or their noses.

Green Eggs and Ham

Saute 1 teaspoon chopped green onions, 1 teaspoon chopped green peppers and 1 tablespoon chopped ham in a pan with a small amount of oil. Stir in 3 teaspoons chopped spinach and add 1 egg that has been mixed with 1 teaspoon milk. Add salt and pepper to taste and stir constantly until egg is set. Makes 1 serving.

I Love Eggs
Sung to: "Frere Jacques"

I love eggs, I love eggs,
Yum, yum, yum, in my tum.
Scrambled, boiled or fried,
Any way I've tried.
Yum, yum, yum; yum, yum, yum.

Jean Warren

Children's Books:
- *Chickens Aren't the Only Ones,*
  Ruth Heller, (Putnam, 1981).
- *Horton Hatches the Egg,* Dr. Seuss,
  (Random, 1940).
- *It Zwibble,* Tom Ross, (Scholastic, 1987).

Contributors:
Susan M. Paprocki, Northbrook, IL

Feet Butterflies

Have each child stand on a piece of paper with feet slightly apart. Trace around each child's feet to make "butterfly wings." Draw a butterfly body between each pair of wings and add antennae and smiling faces. Let the children decorate their butterflies with crayons. Then have them brush glue over their butterflies and sprinkle them with glitter.

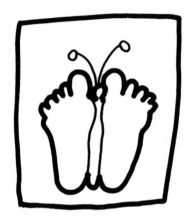

Footprints

Set up an assembly line for this activity. One at a time, have the children remove their shoes and socks and step into a large shallow pan of tempera paint. Help each child carefully step onto and walk across a long strip of butcher paper. Then have the children step into a pan of warm soapy water placed at the end of the paper. Finally, have them walk onto a towel and help them dry off their feet.

Hint: This activity usually requires two or more adults to assist if there are more than five children involved.

Foot Puppets

Have each child stand on a piece of construction paper. Trace around one foot and cut out the shape. Next, glue a tongue depressor to the heel of the foot for a handle. Let the children draw faces on their foot puppets. Then have them answer questions addressed to their puppets. For example: "Where have you walked today? What are your favorite shoes? How high can you jump?"

Dancing Man
Sung to: "This Old Man"

This old man, he has feet,
See him dancing down the street.
With a tip, tap, tip, tap,
Watch him go,
Sometimes fast and sometimes slow.

This old man, he has feet,
See him twirling down the street.
With a tip, tap, tip, tap,
Watch him go,
Sometimes fast and sometimes slow.

Additional verses: "See him leaping down the street; See him jumping down the street; See him marching down the street."

Have the children move their feet or use their foot puppets from the activity above to act out the movements in the song.

Jean Warren

Jumping Feet

Cut right and left foot shapes out of dark colored self-stick paper. Peel the backing off of the shapes and place them on the floor in a pattern. For example, start a simple pattern by placing two feet together, two feet apart, then two feet together. Make progressively difficult patterns with additional foot shapes. Then let the children follow the patterns by jumping from one set of footprints to the next.

Exploring Feet

Have the children sit on the floor and concentrate on their feet. Have them make running motions with their feet, wiggle their toes, move their feet around in circles, tap their feet together and stomp their feet. Next have them stand up and explore with their feet. Have them move with quiet feet, sneaky feet, heavy feet, big feet, tiny feet, fast feet and slow feet. Ask them to show you their walking feet, their running feet, their marching feet, their skipping feet and their jumping feet.

Counting Feet

Cut six egg cups from a cardboard egg carton. Poke a pipe cleaner through each egg cup to make two legs and bend up the ends to make feet. Decorate the last cup with two eyes and two antennae. Have the children place several of the cups in a row to create a caterpillar. Have them count the number of feet it has. Then let them line up a different number of egg cups and count the feet on the new caterpillar they have made.

Foot Pairs

From construction paper cut out several pairs of foot shapes in varying sizes. Mix up the shapes. Have the children find the matching pairs of feet, then arrange them in order from smallest to largest.

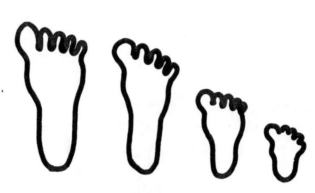

Children's Books:
- *The Foot Book*, Dr. Seuss, (Random, 1968).
- *New Blue Shoes*, Eve Rice, (Penguin, 1979).
- *Shoes*, Elizabeth Winthrop, (Harper, 1986).

Contributors:
Paula Omlin, Maple Valley, WA

Paper Plate Fish

Give each child a paper plate with a triangular mouth shape drawn on one side. Have the children cut out the triangles. (The openings are the mouths of the fish.) Then have them glue the triangular pieces on the opposite sides of their plates to make tails. Let the children complete their fish by drawing on eyes and coloring them as desired.

Extension: Have the children paint a large sheet of butcher paper with diluted blue tempera paint. When the paint is dry, have each child glue his or her fish on the paper "ocean." Hang the ocean mural on a wall or a bulletin board.

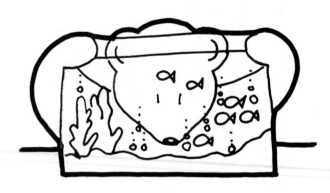

Observing Fish

Set up an aquarium or a bowl of fish at your science table. Make a poster to hang above the aquarium that shows the parts of a fish (body, eyes, fins, gills and tail). Discuss the proper care of fish and let the children take turns with the feeding. Have the children observe the fish and draw pictures of their observations. While discussing their findings, ask questions such as these: "How do fish swim? What are the gills used for? Do fish sleep?"

Sorting Fish

Purchase several different kinds and colors of small plastic fish. Place them all in a basket. Let the children take turns sorting them by color, by shape and by size.

Let's Go Fishing

Make a fishing pole by tying 3 feet of string to a dowel, a paper towel tube or a wooden spoon. Attach a small magnet to the end of the string. Cut fish shapes from different colors of construction paper and attach a paper clip to each fish. Lay the fish shapes out on the floor. Then let the children take turns catching all the red fish, then all the blue fish, etc.

Variation: To play a number game, ask the children to catch five fish, three fish, etc. Or write numbers on the fish shapes and ask the children to catch a "two" fish, a "four" fish, etc.

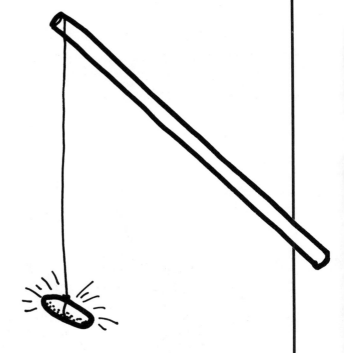

I'm a Little Fishy

Sung to: "I'm a Little Teapot"

I'm a little fishy,
I can swim.
Here is my tail,
Here is my fin.
When I want to have fun
With my friends,
I wiggle my tail and
Dive right in.

Lynn Beaird
Loma Linda, CA

Three Brook Trout

Sung to: "Three Blind Mice"

Three brook trout,
Three brook trout.
See how they swim,
See how they swim.
Their tails go left and
Their tails go right,
Their gills breathe in and
Their gills breathe out,
Did you ever see
Such a slippery sight as
Three brook trout?

Substitute other fish names such as "silver salmon" or "red snapper" for "brook trout."

Barbara Dunn
Hollidaysburg, PA

Five Little Fish

Cut five fish shapes out of felt. Place the shapes on a flannelboard. As you read the poem below, let the children take turns "catching" the fish by removing them from the flannelboard.

Five little fish swimming by the shore.
One got caught, and then there were four.

Four little fish swimming in the sea.
One got caught, and then there were three.

Three little fish swimming in the blue.
One got caught, and then there were two.

Two little fish swimming in the sun.
One got caught, and then there was one.

One little fish swimming for home
Decided 'twas best to never roam.

Jean Warren

Fishy Treats

Give each of the children a large cracker or half a slice of whole-wheat bread. Let them spread on tuna salad or cream cheese mixed with smoked salmon. Top with tiny fish-shaped crackers.

Children's Books:
- *Fish Is Fish,* Leo Lionni, (Knopf, 1970).
- *Louis the Fish,* Arthur Yorinks, (Farrar, Straus & Giroux, 1980).
- *Swimmy,* Leo Lionni, (Knopf, 1963).

Contributors:
Barbara Dunn, Hollidaysburg, PA

GINGERBREAD PEOPLE

Decorating Gingerbread People

Cut gingerbread people shapes out of brown construction paper or brown paper bags. Give one to each child. Have the children decorate their shapes with felt pieces, rickrack, sequins, fabric or paper scraps, buttons, etc.

Variation: Let the children cover their shapes with glue and sprinkle on dried tea leaves or coffee grounds before decorating.

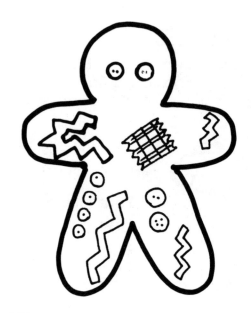

Making Brown Paint

Let the children experiment with mixing together different colors of paint to make the color brown. Then have them use their brown paint to paint giant gingerbread people shapes on pieces of butcher paper. Display their gingerbread people pictures around the room.

Where Is the Gingerbread Man?

Secretly hide a brown paper gingerbread man in the room. Read the story "The Gingerbread Man" to the children. Then tell them about the gingerbread man you have hidden and let them take turns guessing where he might be. Let the child who guesses correctly hide the gingerbread man for a new round of the game or keep him as a prize.

Gingerbread Puppets

Give the children gingerbread people shapes cut out of construction paper. Let the children decorate their shapes with felt-tip markers. Glue their gingerbread people shapes to tongue depressors to make stick puppets. Let the children talk to each other with their puppets or make up questions for their puppets to answer.

GINGERBREAD PEOPLE

Counting Fun

Cut ten small gingerbread people shapes out of felt. Let the children use the shapes on a flannelboard to practice counting.

Gingerbread People Match-Ups

Cut four pairs of gingerbread people shapes out of felt or construction paper. Decorate each pair differently. Then mix up the shapes and let the children take turns finding the matching pairs.

The Gingerbread Man
Sung to: "The Muffin Man"

Oh, do you know the Gingerbread Man,
Gingerbread Man, Gingerbread Man?
Oh, do you know the Gingerbread Man,
Who ran and ran and ran?

He said, "Catch me if you can,
If you can, if you can."
He said, "Catch me if you can,"
Then ran and ran and ran.

I can run like the Gingerbread Man,
Gingerbread Man, Gingerbread Man.
I can run like the Gingerbread Man,
Now catch me if you can.

Jean Warren

Run, Gingerbread Man, Run

Let the children have fun running like the Gingerbread Man in the story. How slowly can they run? How fast? Can they run sideways, backward, quietly, noisily?

Gingerbread Man Cookies

Let the children help you make gingerbread man cookies. Have another adult take the cookies out of the oven when they are done and hide them in a predetermined location. When the children return to the kitchen and see that the cookies have disappeared, let them discover this note on the oven door: "Run, run, as fast as you can. You can't catch me, I'm the Gingerbread Man!" Then search together for the cookies. Once they have been found, let the children decorate them with frosting, raisins, nuts, etc., and enjoy the cookies as snacks.

Children's Books:
- *Gingerbread Boy,* Paul Galdone, (Houghton Mifflin, 1983).
- *What's in the Fox's Sack?,* Paul Galdone, (Clarion, 1982).

Contributors:
Joyce Marshall, Whitby, Ontario
Kathy Monahan, Coon Rapids, MN
Nancy Ridgeway, Bradford, PA

GROUNDHOGS

Groundhog Puppets

Let the children use felt-tip markers to draw groundhog faces on the top halves of tongue depressors. Give them each a small paper cup with a slit in the bottom. Have them push the bottoms of their tongue depressors through the slits in their cups. Show them how to move their sticks up and down to make their groundhogs appear and disappear.

Groundhog Tunnel Game

Have the children line up in a row. (If there are a lot of children, have them line up in two rows.) To form a tunnel, have them stand close together with their legs apart. Let the last person in the row be the first groundhog. Have the first groundhog wiggle through the tunnel on his or her stomach. When the groundhog reaches the end of the tunnel, have him or her stand up and become a part of the tunnel while a new groundhog starts wiggling through.

Shadow Tag

Let the children play shadow tag on a sunny day. Choose a child to be ''It.'' Have ''It'' try to step on another child's shadow. When ''It'' steps on someone's shadow, that child becomes the next ''It.''

I'm a Little Groundhog
Sung to: "I'm a Little Teapot"

I'm a little groundhog,
Furry and brown.
When winter comes
I sleep underground.
I'm curled up
As cozy as can be.
When it's spring,
Please wake up me!

Colraine Pettipaw Hunley
Doylestown, PA

Nine Little Groundhogs
Sung to: "Ten Little Indians"

One little, two little,
Three little groundhogs,
Four little, five little,
Six little groundhogs,
Seven little, eight little,
Nine little groundhogs,
Sleeping down under the ground.

Have fun singing this song with loud
voices, with "inside" voices, with whisper
voices and then with "lip" voices (lips
move but no sound comes out).

Colraine Pettipaw Hunley
Doylestown, PA

If I Saw My Shadow
Have the children draw pictures of what they would do if they were groundhogs and saw their shadows on February 2. Ask them one at a time to describe their pictures as you write down their stories on their papers.

Mr. Groundhog

Folklore has it that on February 2, Mr. Groundhog wakes up from his long winter's nap and goes outside. They say that if he sees his shadow, he runs back inside his hole to sleep, indicating that there will be six more weeks of winter. If Mr. Groundhog does not see his shadow he stays outside to play, which means that spring will soon arrive. Let the children take turns being Mr. Groundhog popping out of his hole (a large cardboard box) while everyone recites the poem below.

Hint: Arrange your room so that you can create or take away a shadow. Overhead lights would eliminate a shadow and a low light aimed directly at the ''groundhog'' would create a shadow.

Groundhog, Groundhog, popping up today.
Groundhog, Groundhog, can you play?
If you see your shadow, hide away.
If there is no shadow, you can stay.
Groundhog, Groundhog, popping up today.
Groundhog, Groundhog, can you play?

Jean Warren

Shadow Making

Explain to the children that shadows are caused by objects that get in the way of the sun or a bright light. Shine the light from a film projector, a slide projector or a lamp on a bare wall. Turn off the lights in the room. Let the children stand in front of the bright light and experiment with making their own shadows. Ask them to make big shadows, little shadows, animal shadows and moving shadows.

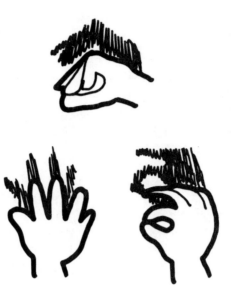

Groundhog Lunches

Groundhogs like to nibble on grasses and other greens that grow near their burrows. For "groundhog lunches" let the children help make watercress and romaine lettuce salads to eat with a favorite dressing.

Children's Books:
- *Will Spring Be Early or Will Spring Be Late?*, Crockett Johnson, (Harper, 1959).

Contributors:
Colraine Pettipaw Hunley, Doylestown, PA

Hand Pictures

Mix tempera paint to the consistency of cream and spread it on a sheet of plastic. Let the children place their hands in the paint and then decorate pieces of construction paper with handprints.

Variation: An upside-down handprint makes a nice "Christmas tree," and two overlapped handprints make a pretty "heart."

Musical Fingers

Select a variety of music to play. Give the children large pieces of paper with spoonfuls of fingerpaint placed in the centers. Play the music and let the children fingerpaint to it. Encourage them to move their fingers and hands to the rhythms and tempos of the different kinds of music.

Hand Coupons

Have the children each make handprints on four or five sheets of paper. Staple the papers together and let the children give them to family members or friends as gift coupon books. Recipients can tear out the pages and present them to the children when they need helping hands.

Big Hands, Little Hands

Cut a big hand shape and a little hand shape out of each of the following colors of construction paper: red, blue, green, yellow, orange and purple. Put the shapes in a pile. Let the children take turns matching the hands by color or sorting them by size.

See What We Can Do

Read the following poem to the children. Have them listen carefully and move their hands as described in the poem.

Hands, hands, hands, hands,
See what we can do.
Hands, hands, hands, hands,
See what we can do.

Shake, shake, shake, shake,
That's what we can do.
Shake, shake, shake, shake,
That's what we can do.

Clap, clap, clap, clap,
That's what we can do.
Clap, clap, clap, clap,
That's what we can do.

Snap, snap, snap, snap,
That's what we can do.
Snap, snap, snap, snap,
That's what we can do.

Author Unknown

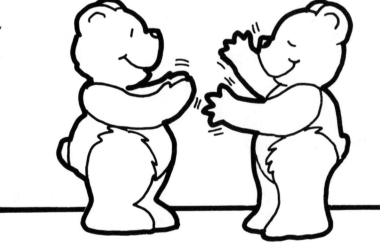

This Old Hand

Sung to: "This Old Man"

This old hand, finger one,
It's the same as my thumb.
With a nick-nack paddy-wack,
Give a dog a bone.
This old hand is going home.

This old hand, finger two,
I can place it on my shoe.
With a nick-nack paddy-wack,
Give a dog a bone.
This old hand is going home.

This old hand, finger three,
I can place it on my knee.
With a nick-nack paddy-wack,
Give a dog a bone.
This old hand is going home.

This old hand, finger four,
I can tap it on the floor.
With a nick-nack paddy-wack,
Give a dog a bone.
This old hand is going home.

This old hand, finger five,
It's the baby by its size.
With a nick-nack paddy-wack,
Give a dog a bone.
This old hand is going home.

Jean Warren

Roll, Roll, Roll Your Hands

Sung to: "Row, Row, Row Your Boat"

Roll, roll, roll your hands,
Slowly as can be.
Roll them slow as you go,
Roll them one, two, three.

Roll, roll, roll your hands,
Fast as fast can be.
Roll them fast, don't be last,
Roll them one, two, three.

Additional verses: "Clap, clap, clap your
hands; Wave, wave, wave your hands;
Tap, tap, tap your hands."

Adapted Traditional

Exploring Hands

Have the children examine their hands. Then let them experiment with different ways of moving their hands, fingers and wrists. Have them stand still and see how far out and how far up and down they can stretch their hands. How would they use their hands to pick up something heavy? Could they lift it high over their heads? How would they pick up something slimy, something sticky or something round? Can they make their hands look like gentle hands, mean hands, strong hands, weak hands, working hands or playful hands?

Children's Books:

- *Here Are My Hands*, Bill Martin, (Henry Holt, 1987).
- *If You're Happy and You Know It*, Nicki Weiss, (Greenwillow, 1987).
- *The Mitten*, Alvin Tresselt, (Scholastic, 1985).

Finger Foods

Provide carrot sticks, apple slices and cheese sticks for the children to eat with their fingers at snacktime.

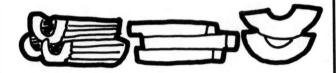

Hand Cookies

Use a favorite recipe to make cookies and let the children help roll out the cookie dough. Place the children's hands on the dough and trace around them. Then cut out the shapes and use a toothpick to write the children's names on their hand cookies. Bake according to your recipe directions.

Contributors:

Ann Herold-Short, Rushville, IN
Debbie Jones, Richland, WA

Decorating Hats

Make hats for the children by cutting the centers out of paper plates and stapling paper soup bowls over the holes. Attach yarn to the sides of the hats for ties. Then let the children decorate their hats with materials such as feathers, sequins, fabric scraps, ribbon, artificial flowers, glitter and yarn.

Variation: Instead of paper plate hats, make cone-shaped hats from construction paper or folded paper hats from newsprint.

Hat Collages

Let the children find pictures of hats in old magazines. Then let them cut or tear out the pictures and glue them to precut hat shapes. Display their hat collages around the room.

When March Hats Blow

Cut nine different hat shapes out of felt, one each from blue, yellow, red, brown, green, black, orange, white and purple. Place the hat shapes on the left side of a flannelboard. As you recite the poem, "fly" the appropriate colored hats across the flannelboard to the right side. Then repeat the poem and let the children help decide the order of the colors.

When I hear the March winds blow,
I look up in the sky.
Instead of things like birds or planes,
I watch the hats fly by.

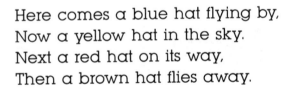

Each one different from the last,
Every color do I see.
Some are big and some are small,
As they fly by me.

Here comes a blue hat flying by,
Now a yellow hat in the sky.
Next a red hat on its way,
Then a brown hat flies away.

Green and black, orange and white,
Even purple – what a sight!
I like it when there's rain and snow,
But most of all when March hats blow.

Jean Warren

What Can I Be?

Collect hats from a variety of occupations such as construction worker, firefighter, police officer, chef, cowhand, baseball player and clown. Place the hats in a pile. Let the children take turns selecting a hat to wear while you sing the following song.

Sung to: "Row, Row, Row Your Boat"

What, what can you be
With a hat like that?
You could be a _____.
With a hat like that.

Cindy Dingwall
Palatine, IL

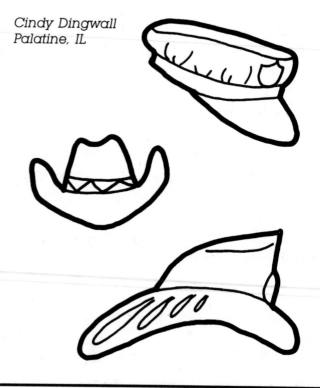

Keep It Under Your Hat

This game works well during circle time. Hide a small object under a hat. Give the children clues about the object and have them try guessing what the object is. As the children learn how to describe objects, they can take turns hiding the objects and giving the clues themselves.

Fun With Hats

Make a large number of cone hats in a variety of sizes and colors. Let the children use the hats in different combinations to play the games below.

△ Select a number from a hat and stack that number of cone hats in a pile.

△ Sort the hats by color or by size.

△ Arrange a few hats in order from smallest to largest.

△ Place the hats on stuffed animals by matching small hats to small animals and large hats to large animals.

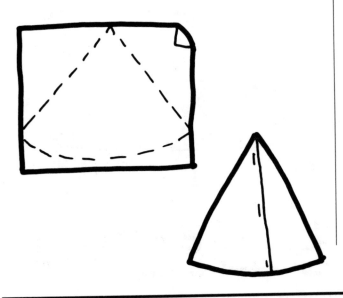

Matching Hats and Colors

Draw six pairs of different kinds of hats on twelve index cards. Color three of the hats red, three yellow, three blue and three green. If desired, cover the cards with clear self-stick paper for durability. Put the cards in a pile and let the children take turns matching the hats by kind or by color.

Hat Parade

Let the children show off their decorated hats by joining in a Hat Parade. Sing the following song while the children circle around the room.

Sung to: "The Mulberry Bush"

Here we go round in a Hat Parade,
A Hat Parade, a Hat Parade.
Here we go round in a Hat Parade,
Look at our fancy hats.

Here comes (child's name) with a fancy hat.
A fancy hat, a fancy hat,
Here comes (child's name) with a fancy hat,
Oh, what a grand parade!

Susan M. Paprocki
Northbrook, IL

Hat Charades

Set out a box filled with different kinds of hats. Let the children take turns selecting a hat from the box and acting out what a person who wears that kind of hat does.

Musical Hats

Have the children sit in a circle. Place several hats in the middle. Let one child select a hat and put it on. Begin playing music. Have the child wearing the hat remove it and place it on the head of the next child. Let the children continue passing the hat in this manner. When you stop the music, have the child wearing the hat put it in the middle of the circle and select a new hat. Start the music again and let the children pass the new hat. Continue until each child has had a chance to select a hat.

Children's Books:
- *Caps for Sale*, Esphyr Slobodkina, (Harper, 1947).
- *Martin's Hats*, Joan Blos, (Macmillan, 1987).

Hat Dance

Place a sombrero (or any kind of large hat) on the floor and let the children dance around it as they sing the song below. For a festive touch let them wear sashes made of colored crepe paper streamers around their waists.

Sung to: "La Raspa"
(Mexican Hat Dance Song)

Let's dance and dance and dance,
Around the hat let's dance.
Let's dance and dance and dance,
Around the hat let's dance.

Tra-la-la-la-la-la-la-la-la-la
Tra-la-la-la-la-la-la-la-la-la,
Tra-la-la-la-la-la-la-la-la-la,
Around the hat let's dance.

Jean Warren

Contributors:
Cindy Dingwall, Palatine, IL
Susan M. Paprocki, Northbrook, IL

Ink Hearts

Draw large heart outlines on white paper towels with a black non-permanent felt-tip marker. Let the children brush water over the heart outlines to reveal the other colors contained in the black ink.

Heart Fold-Overs

For each child cut various sizes of heart shapes out of white construction paper and fold them in half. Let the children lay their hearts out flat and place drops of red, pink and lavender tempera paint on one side. Have them fold their hearts and rub the tops with their hands. Then let them open their heart shapes to see the beautiful designs they have created.

Heart Rubbings

Cut hearts out of a variety of textured materials (sandpaper, corrugated cardboard, wallpaper, needlework canvas, etc.). Let the children make heart rubbings by placing the hearts under sheets of paper and rubbing across their papers with crayons.

Heart Bears

For each child cut out one brown construction paper bear shape, five small red construction paper hearts to glue on the paws and nose and one large heart to glue on the chest. Then let the children glue the hearts on their bears to make ''Beary Happy Valentines.''

Heart Prints

Have the children brush white vinegar on white construction paper. Then let them cover their papers with precut red tissue paper hearts. As the vinegar dries, the tissue paper will fall off, leaving red heart prints.

Rhyming Hearts

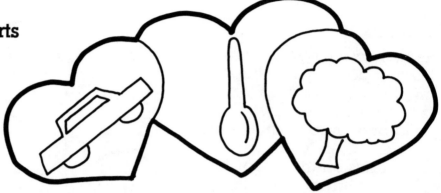

Cut out ten to twenty red construction paper hearts and glue a magazine picture on each one. Place the hearts in a paper bag and let the children take turns drawing one out. Have the children name words that rhyme with the names of the pictures on the hearts. When all of the hearts have been drawn, have the children place them back in the bag and start all over again.

This Little Heart

Attach heart stickers to the fingers of each child's right or left hand before reciting the poem below.

This little heart is here to say
   (Wiggle thumb.)
That this little heart loves you today.
   (Wiggle index finger.)
These little hearts
   (Wiggle next three fingers.)
Wish Mom, Dad and you
A terrific Valentine's Day, through and through.

Betty Silkunas
Lansdale, PA

Heart Puzzles

Cut eight to twelve heart shapes out of posterboard or construction paper. Cut each heart into a different two-piece puzzle. Let the children take turns putting the heart puzzles together.

Variation: For beginning puzzles, make each one a different color.

Heart Match-Ups

For each child cut a heart out of red or pink construction paper. Cut each heart in half differently and place the halves in separate piles. Give each child a half from one pile and hide the other halves around the room. Then let the children have fun hunting for the matching halves of their hearts.

Variation: Use one heart for every two children. Cut the hearts into two pieces and give each child a half. Use this game as a mixer or for choosing partners for another activity.

Heart Hunt

Hide twenty or more small red hearts around the room. Then let the children have a "heart hunt." The person who finds the most hearts gets to be King or Queen of Hearts for the day. Make sure everyone finds some hearts.

Heart Box Puzzle

Trace around a heart-shaped candy box on a piece of red or pink construction paper or posterboard. Cut out the heart shape, then cut it into puzzle pieces. Then let the children take turns using the box as a puzzle holder while putting the pieces of the heart together.

I've Got a Big Red Heart

Sung to: "For He's a Jolly Good Fellow"

I've got a big red heart,
I've got a big red heart,
I've got a big red heart
That I will give to you.

It brings you love and kisses,
It brings you love and kisses,
It brings you love and kisses
Because you are my friend.

Maureen Gutyan
Williams Lake, B.C.

I'm a Happy Little Heart

Sung to: "Little White Duck"

I'm a happy little heart
That's pink and white and red,
A happy little heart
With lace around my edge.
I have three words
On the front of me
That say "I love you,"
Oh, can't you see?
I'm a happy little heart
That's pink and white and red.
Happy little heart!

Gayle Bittinger

Heart Waffles

Toast frozen waffles and let the children use cookie cutters to cut them into heart shapes. Then let the children decorate their waffle hearts with powdered sugar.

Betty Silkunas
Lansdale, PA

Red Gelatin Hearts

In a saucepan bring to a boil 1 cup unsweetened frozen apple juice concentrate and 1 cup water. Sprinkle 2 envelopes plain gelatin and 1 teaspoon unsweetened raspberry Kool-Aid mix into a bowl. Pour in the heated liquid ingredients and stir until gelatin is dissolved. Pour the mixture into a rectangular cake pan that has been sprayed with nonstick vegetable cooking spray. Chill until set. Then use a cookie cutter to cut heart shapes in the gelatin and lift them out carefully with a spatula. Arrange the hearts on top of lettuce leaves placed on small plates and top with mayonnaise and chopped walnuts, if desired. Makes approximately 12 hearts.

Heart Cake

Use your favorite recipe to prepare cake batter. Pour the batter into one round pan and one square pan. Make a large platter for the cake by covering a large piece of cardboard with foil. Place the square cake on the platter with one corner facing downward. Then cut the round cake in half and place the halves against the top two sides of the square cake to make a heart shape. Cover the entire cake with pink frosting and decorate it as desired.

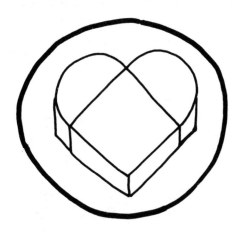

Heart Straws

Turn ordinary drinking straws into party straws by sliding on small valentines. Use purchased valentines or make your own out of red and white construction paper. Fold each valentine in half vertically and make a horizontal ½-inch slit near the top and another one near the bottom. Then slide a straw in one slit and out the other.

Children's Books:
- *Hear Your Heart*, Paul Showers, (Harper, 1968).
- *Valentine Bears*, Eve Bunting, (Houghton Mifflin, 1983).
- *Valentine's Day*, Gail Gibbon, (Holiday House, 1986).

Contributors:
Cathy Griffin, Princeton Junction, NJ
Barb Mazzochi, Villa Park, IL
Betty Silkunas, Lansdale, PA

LEAVES

Fall Leaf Hangings

Set out a variety of colorful fall leaves. Give each child a 6- to 10-inch square of clear self-stick paper with the backing removed. Let the children arrange the leaves on the sticky sides of their squares. When each child is finished, place a second clear self-stick paper square (with the backing removed) over the first square and seal the edges well. Punch a hole at the top of each square and add a loop of yarn. Arrange the leaf hangings in a window. When the sun shines through, they will sparkle with color!

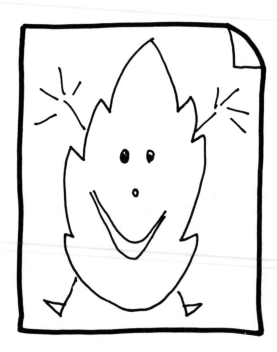

Leaf Creatures

Give the children construction paper, glue, felt-tip markers and an assortment of colorful fall leaves. Have each child select two or three leaves and glue them on his or her paper. Let the children use felt-tip markers to add arms, legs, hands, feet, hair, eyes and other features to make leaf creatures.

Leaf Frames

For each child you will need two clear plastic lids that are the same size (coffee can lids, margarine tub lids, etc.). Cut the outer rim off of one lid so that it will fit snugly inside the other lid. Collect a variety of autumn leaves. Let the children each choose one or two leaves and glue them inside their rimmed lids. Then have them put their rimless lids on top of their leaves and snap them in place. Attach ribbons to the tops of the finished leaf frames and hang them in a window.

Leaf Decorations

On large pieces, of paper, let the children fingerpaint with bright fall colors or paint with watercolors. When the paint has dried, cut leaf shapes out of the papers. Use the brightly colored leaves to decorate your room.

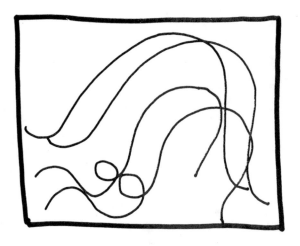

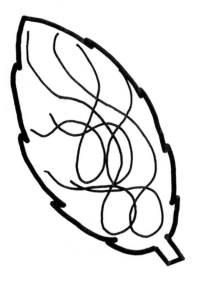

Leaf Creature Stories

After the children have completed their leaf creatures from the activity on page 152, ask them to tell you stories about their creatures. Write each story at the bottom of the storyteller's paper. With the permission of the author, read each story out loud to the whole group.

Leaf-Word Matching

Collect five samples of different kinds of leaves. Mount each leaf on a piece of lightweight cardboard, print its name on the cardboard and cover the entire piece with clear self-stick paper. Make five corresponding word cards by printing the name of each leaf on a separate card and covering it with clear self-stick paper. Have the children match the word cards with the corresponding leaf-and-word cards.

Leaf Pairs

Collect six pairs of different kinds of fall leaves. Press the leaves between heavy books for several days. Mount each leaf on an index card and cover the cards with clear self-stick paper. Then let the children take turns matching the pairs of leaves.

Extension: If you have a large supply of leaves, let the children make their own leaf pairs.

Sorting Leaves

Choose three or four leaves with common shapes and tape each one to a different box. Set out a number of matching shaped leaves. Then let the children take turns choosing a leaf and placing it in the appropriate box.

Leaf Matching

Collect five good-sized leaves. Trace each of their outlines on a separate piece of paper. Challenge the children to match each leaf to its outline. (This activity must be used the same day it is prepared; as the leaves dry, they will curl up and no longer fit their original outlines.)

How Many Leaves?

Place several fall leaves in a see-through container such as a glass jar or a clear plastic bag. Ask the children to guess how many leaves are inside. Then take out the leaves and count them together. Were the children's guesses too high or too low? Place a different number of leaves in the container and have the children guess and count again.

Autumn Leaf Express

Use colorful autumn leaves to teach and reinforce color skills. Take the children outside to an area with lots of autumn leaves on the ground. Tell the children that you are the conductor of the Autumn Leaf Express. In order to ride on your train, they must each find a leaf that is the color you announce. When you say "All aboard the Yellow Leaf Express," have the children find yellow leaves, hook on behind you and "choo-choo" around the area. Stop the train, announce a new color, have the children collect new leaves and begin the fun again.

Fall Leaves

Let the children act out the appropriate movements as you recite the following poem.

Down, down,
Yellow and brown,
Fall the leaves
All over the ground.
Rake them up
In a pile so high,
They almost reach
Up to the sky.

Traditional

Leaf Graphing

Prepare a simple graph by drawing a grid on a large piece of paper. Glue a different colored leaf in each of the left-hand squares on the grid. Set out a variety of matching colored leaves and have the children sort them by color. Then count all the leaves of one color together with the children. Find the matching colored leaf on the graph and mark off one square for each leaf of that color. Continue until all the leaves have been counted.

Variation: Make a graph to count leaf shapes instead of leaf colors.

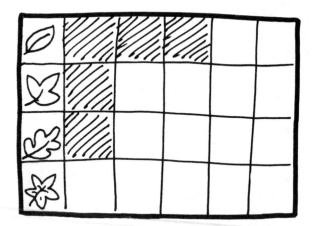

Autumn Leaves All Around Me
Sung to: "Mary Had a Little Lamb"

Autumn leaves all around me,
All around me, all around me.
Autumn leaves all around me,
What colors do you see?

Red and yellow, gold and brown,
Gold and brown, gold and brown.
Red and yellow, gold and brown,
Falling gracefully.

Susan M. Paprocki
Northbrook, IL

The Leaves Are Falling Down
Sung to: "The Farmer in the Dell"

The leaves are falling down,
The leaves are falling down.
School is here and
Fall is near,
The leaves are falling down.

The leaves are falling down,
The leaves are falling down.
Some are red and
Some are brown,
The leaves are falling down.

The leaves are falling down,
The leaves are falling down.
They tickle your nose and
Touch your toes,
The leaves are falling down.

June Haggard
Lake Geneva, WI

Leaves, Leaves
Sung to: "Row, Row, Row Your Boat"

Leaves, leaves falling down,
(Wiggle fingers downward.)
Falling on the ground.
Red and yellow,
Orange and brown,
Leaves are falling down.

Susan A. Miller
Kutztown, PA

Children's Books:
- *Fall of Freddie the Leaf*, Leo Buscaglia, (Henry Holt, 1982).
- *Tree Is Nice*, Janice Udry, (Harper Row, 1956).
- *Why Do Leaves Change Color?*, Chris Arvetis, (Rand McNally, 1986).

Contributors:
Jean Hack, Bedford, OH
Colraine Pettipaw Hunley, Doylestown, PA
Debbie Jones, Richland, WA
Betty Silkunas, Lansdale, PA
Kristine Wagoner, Pacific, WA

Lion Puppets

Give the children paper plates, glue, 2-inch pieces of yellow yarn and felt-tip markers. Have them make lion manes by gluing yarn pieces around the rims of their paper plates. Then let them draw lion faces on the centers of their plates with felt-tip markers. Attach Popsicle stick handles to the backs of the plates to make lion puppets.

Lamb Puppets

Set out paper plates, cotton balls, glue and felt-tip markers. Have the children glue cotton ball "wool" around the rims of their paper plates. When they have finished, let them draw lamb faces on the centers of their plates with felt-tip markers. Attach Popsicle stick handles to the backs of the plates to make lamb puppets.

Opposites

Use the saying "March comes in like a lion and goes out like a lamb" as a basis for discussing opposites. Older children may understand the meaning behind the saying. Younger children will be more interested in talking about loud lions and quiet lambs. Ask the children to "roar" loudly and "baa" quietly. Can they tell you about times when they must be quiet and times when they can be loud?

Loud and Soft Sounds

Go around your house or school with a tape recorder and record loud and soft sounds. Play the tape for the children. Have them tell you what each sound is and whether it is "loud" or "soft." Some examples might be a door banging, water running, a baby crying, soft music playing, a telephone ringing and a bird chirping.

Extension: Ask the children to imagine that they are at the beach, in a car, at school, at the grocery store, etc. Have them name a loud sound and a soft sound they might hear at each place.

LIONS & LAMBS

Winds and Breezes

Give the children light blue crepe paper streamers to hold in their hands. Let them take turns racing across the room and flapping their streamers like strong ''lion'' winds. Then have them walk back across the room, gently waving their streamers like soft ''lamb'' breezes.

Extension: Have the children dance to fast and slow music while holding their streamers.

Like a Lion
Sung to: ''Mary Had a Little Lamb''

March comes in like a lion,
Like a lion, like a lion.
March comes in like a lion,
And goes out like a lamb.

March comes in with a great big wind,
Great big wind, great big wind.
March comes in with a great big wind,
And goes out with a breeze.

June Meckel
Andover, MA

Lion Salads

Place pineapple rings on small plates to use as lion heads. Let the children add shredded carrots for manes, cherries for noses and raisins for eyes.

Lamb Salads

To make each lamb salad, place a mound of cottage cheese in the middle of a small plate. Flatten it with the back of a spoon and make a hollow in the center for the lamb's face. Let the children add raisins for eyes and halves of red grapes or cherry tomatoes for noses.

Children's Books:
- *Dandelion*, Don Freeman, (Viking, 1964).
- *Happy Lion*, Louise Fatio, (Scholastic, 1986).
- *Lamb and the Butterfly*, Arnold Sundgaard, (Orchard, 1988).

Contributors:
Sharon Olson, Minot, ND

Evaporated Milk Paint

Place small amounts of evaporated milk in several small containers. (A six-cup muffin tin works well for this.) Add two or three drops of different colors of food coloring to each container and stir. Let the children use the colored milk to paint on shapes cut out of construction paper.

Variation: Mix food coloring with condensed milk to make enamel-like paint. Let the children use the paint to make stripes of different colors on construction paper squares and then hold up their squares to let the colors run together. (Although this method is expensive, the brilliant colors created make it worth doing at least once a year.)

Ice-Cream Cones

For each child cut a large cone shape out of white construction paper and three circles out of colored construction paper. Have the children place their cone shapes on pieces of plastic screen (or any material that will make criss-cross impressions) and rub across them with brown crayons. Then have each child glue his or her cone shape on a piece of paper and select three colored circles to glue on top to make a triple-decker ice-cream cone.

Making Butter

Fill baby food jars half full of whipping cream and screw the lids on tightly. Let two children take turns shaking each jar. After about six minutes the cream will be whipped, and after another minute or so, lumps of yellow butter will form. Rinse off the liquid whey and add a little salt (if desired) before spreading the butter on crackers for tasting.

Variation: Let the children observe as you use an electric mixer or an egg beater to whip the cream in a bowl. Stop for tasting. Then continue whipping the cream until butter forms.

Count the Cheese Holes

Cut at least six triangles of "cheese" out of yellow construction paper. With a hole punch, punch one hole in the first piece of cheese, two holes in the second piece and so on. Then number six paper plates from 1 to 6. Let the children take turns arranging the paper plates in numerical order. Then have them count the number of holes in the pieces of cheese and place them on the matching numbered plates.

Ice-Cream Cone Match-Ups

Draw identical double-decker ice-cream cones on ten small white index cards. Color each pair a different color. Then mix up the cards and let the children take turns finding the matching pairs of cones.

Thank You, Cows

Sung to: "Mary Had a Little Lamb"

Thank you, cows,
For the milk we drink,
Milk we drink, milk we drink.
Thank you, cows,
For the milk we drink.
We say MOOO to you!

Additional verses: "Thank you, cows, for the butter on our bread; for the cheese on our crackers; for the cream on our pies; for cottage cheese and yogurt; for the ice cream we love."

Elizabeth McKinnon

Cheese Kabobs

Cut several varieties of cheese into 1-inch cubes. Set out the cheese cubes and pretzel sticks. Let the children spear the cubes of cheese on the pretzel sticks to make cheese kabobs.

Purple Cows

In a blender container put 1 cup milk, ¼ cup grape juice and 1 sliced banana. Blend until smooth and frothy. Makes 2 servings.

Cottage Cheese Dip

Blend ⅓ cup milk, 1 pint cottage cheese and ½ package onion or vegetable soup mix by hand or in a blender. Refrigerate ½ hour. Serve with raw vegetables such as carrot and celery sticks, zucchini and cucumber slices or small pieces of cauliflower.

Children's Books:
- *Don't Forget the Bacon!*, Pat Hutchins, (Greenwillow, 1976).
- *Milk and Cookies*, Frank Asch, (Parents, 1982).
- *Milk Makers*, Gail Gibbons, (Macmillan, 1985).

Sun Visors

Give each child a large paper plate with a hole cut out of the middle. Let the children decorate the rims of their paper plates with crayons or felt-tip markers. When they have finished, help them slip their personally designed sun visors over their heads.

Self-Portraits

Set out paper plates to use for faces, various colors of yarn scraps for hair, different colored construction paper circles for eyes and funny hat shapes cut from wallpaper samples or fabric pieces. Have the children take turns looking at themselves in a hand mirror. Ask them to notice the colors of their hair and eyes. Then let them make self-portraits by gluing yarn "hair" and paper "eyes" that match their own hair and eye colors on paper plates. Have the children complete their self-portraits by adding noses and mouths with felt-tip markers and gluing on funny hat shapes. Hang their paper plate faces from the ceiling all around the room.

Feelings

Give each child two paper plates and two or three felt-tip markers. Have each child draw a happy face on one plate and a sad face on the other. Sit together in a group and ask the children to raise their happy faces when you say something that makes them happy and their sad faces when you say something that makes them sad. You might start with such statements as these: "Today is my birthday; I fell off my bike; Susie shared her orange with me; I couldn't play outside today."

Food Collages

Discuss healthy foods with the children. (Depending on the ages of the children, you may also wish to discuss the four food groups — fruits and vegetables, dairy products, meat products and breads.) Have the children search through old magazines and tear or cut out pictures of healthy foods. Then have them glue their nutritious food pictures on paper plates.

Counting Game

For each child use a felt-tip marker to divide a paper plate into four to eight sections (depending on the age of the child). Number the sections on each plate, starting with 1. Set out bowls of dried beans (or other small counting objects). Then have the children identify the numbers on their plates and place the corresponding number of beans in each section.

Puzzle Plates

Give each child a paper plate with a solid color painted around the rim. Let the children use felt-tip markers to draw pictures on their plates. Then cut each plate into three to six puzzle pieces (depending on the age of the child). Give the children their puzzle pieces and plain paper plates to use as puzzle holders. Let the children put their own puzzles together. Then have them exchange puzzles with friends.

Color Match

Paint paper plates (one for every two children) a variety of colors. Cut the plates in half and give each child one piece. Have the children sit in a circle. Let one child begin by holding up his or her colored plate piece. Ask the child with the matching colored piece to hold up his or her plate half. Then ask the group to identify the color of the plate. Continue around the circle until everyone has had a turn.

Finger Puppet Theater

Cut a horizontal slit in the center of a paper plate, leaving about 2½ inches uncut on each side. Make a 1-inch vertical cut at each end of the slit. Use felt-tip markers to draw a scene on the plate, such as a home, a farm, a school or a store. To use the theater, insert a finger puppet through the back of the slit to perform "on stage."

Children's Books:
- *Alligator Arrived With Apples: A Potluck Alphabet Feast,* Crescent Dragonwagon, (Macmillan, 1987).
- *It's Your Turn, Roger!,* Susanna Gretz, (Dial, 1985).
- *Tight Times,* Barbara Hazen, (Viking, 1979).

Contributors:
Colraine Pettipaw Hunley, Doylestown, PA
Susan M. Paprocki, Northbrook, IL
Barbara Robinson, Glendale, AZ

Peanut Butter Playdough

Mix together equal amounts of peanut butter and dry nonfat milk to make playdough (add more peanut butter or dry milk as needed). Wash cookie cutters and any other playing utensils you wish to use and set them out on a clean tabletop. Then invite the children to touch, smell, taste and create with this different kind of playdough.

Variation: For a sweeter taste, mix honey with the peanut butter before adding the dry milk.

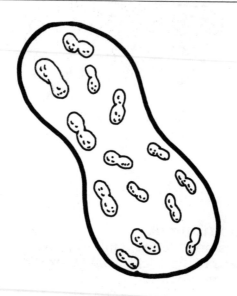

Peanut Shell Collages

Use this activity at the end of your peanut unit to recycle the peanut shells saved from other activities. Cut peanut shapes out of heavy brown grocery sacks or brown construction paper. Pour glue into shallow containers and set out bowls of peanut shells. Then let the children dip the shells into the glue (rounded sides up) and place them all over their peanut shapes to create collages.

The Peanut Plant

Read the following poem with the children. Encourage them to act out the growth of a peanut plant as described. At the end of the poem, ask them to name things they like to eat that are made from the plump and round peanuts.

Up through the ground the peanut plant grows.
   (Crouch down near floor.)
Peeking out its little green nose.
   (Slowly start to rise.)
Reaching, reaching for the sky,
   (Raise arms above head.)
Growing, growing, growing high.
   (Stand on tiptoe.)
Then the flower starts to grow,
   (Make a circle with arms.)
But it doesn't grow up! Not it! Oh, no!
   (Shake head.)
Down it goes, sending shoots underground,
   (Bend over and touch floor with fingers.)
And there grow the peanuts, plump and round.
   (Kneel and pretend to dig up peanuts.)

Author Unknown

Peanut Number Game

Set out five containers numbered from 1 to 5 and a basket containing fifteen peanuts. Then let the children take turns placing the appropriate number of peanuts into each container.

PEANUTS

How Peanuts Grow

Discuss with the children how peanuts grow. Explain that although we think of peanuts as nuts, they really belong to the same family as peas and beans. When a raw peanut is planted, a sprout forms between the two halves of the nut and grows into a flowering plant. Then when the flowers fade, they send shoots down under the ground where the peanut pods form on the ends of the shoots. If possible, show a picture of a peanut plant from an illlustrated dictionary or encyclopedia.

Peanut Drop

To develop color discrimination and eye-hand coordination skills, mark unshelled peanuts with different colored felt-tip markers. Tape matching colors of construction paper to wide-mouthed containers placed on the floor. Then let the children take turns standing beside the containers and dropping matching colored peanuts into each one.

Variation: Number the containers and let the children take turns dropping in the corresponding numbers of peanuts while everyone counts.

Found a Peanut

Hide peanuts in the room in advance (enough so that every child will be successful in finding several) and let the children have a "peanut hunt" while singing the following song.

Sung to: "Oh, My Darling Clementine"

Found a peanut, found a peanut,
Found a peanut just now.
Just now I found a peanut,
Found a peanut just now.

Traditional

Feed the Elephant

Draw an elephant face on the side of a large cardboard box and cut out a hole for its mouth with a sharp knife. Give each of the children several unshelled peanuts and let them take turns "feeding the elephant" by tossing the peanuts into the elephant's mouth. Add more peanuts to the box at the end of the game and let each child reach in and grab a handful. Let the children keep and eat as many peanuts as they can hold.

A Peanut Sat on a Railroad Track
Sung to: "Pop! Goes the Weasel"

A peanut sat on a railroad track,
Its heart was all a-flutter.
A train came chugging down the track —
Whoops! Peanut butter!

Adapted Traditional

Peanut Butter
Sung to: "Frere Jacques"

Peanut butter, peanut butter,
Good for you, fun to chew.
Put peanuts in a blender,
Add a little oil.
Let it whirl, let it swirl.

Peanut butter, peanut butter,
Now it's done; oh, what fun!
Spread it on a sandwich,
Spread it on a cracker.
Good for you, fun to chew.

Susan Peters
Upland, CA

Peanut Butter

Let the children help shell a package of unsalted, roasted peanuts. Then have them grind the peanuts in a food grinder. Gradually add peanuts or vegetable oil until the mixture is the desired consistency. Add salt to taste. Serve on crackers, apple slices or celery sticks. Or, for a special treat, spread on slices of whole-wheat toast and top with warm applesauce.

Nutty Bananas

Finely chop some peanuts. Give each child a plate with a small amount of chopped peanuts, a spoonful of yogurt and one half of an unpeeled banana on it. Have the children gradually peel their bananas and dip them first into the yogurt and then into the nuts before taking each bite.

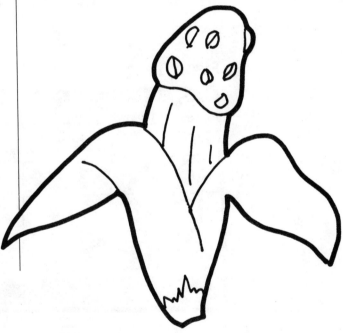

Children's Books:
- *Frederick*, Leo Lionni, (Knopf, 1987).
- *Peanut Butter and Jelly: A Play Rhyme*, Nadine Westcott, (Dutton, 1987).

Contributors:
Judi Repko, Topton, PA
Rosemary Spatafora, Pleasant Ridge, MI

Pizza Collages

For each child cut a large yellow circle "pizza" and the following "toppings" out of construction paper: small red circles for tomatoes; brown circles for sausages; white spirals for onions; black ovals for olives; green squares for peppers; white mushroom shapes for mushrooms. Then give the children their pizzas and let them glue on their choice of toppings.

Graphing Pizza Toppings

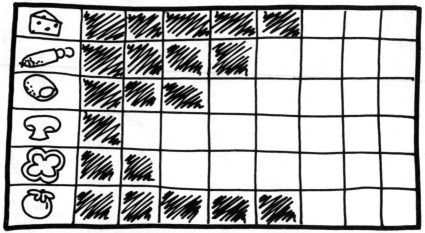

Make a graph with a list of pizza toppings on the left side and blank spaces for tallying on the right. Conduct a survey of the children to find out which pizza toppings they like. Name a topping from the list and ask the children who like that topping to raise their hands. Help the children count the number of hands raised, then mark off that many squares on the graph. Repeat for each topping. Then ask the children to decide which topping is the most popular and which is the least.

Pizza Toppings Game

Play a fun language game by letting the children name toppings they like on their pizzas. Have the first child begin by saying, "I'm going to make a pizza with _____." Have the second child repeat what the first child said and add the name of his or her favorite topping to the end of the sentence. Continue until every child has had a chance to add a topping name to the list.

Hint: Use age and ability to determine when to start the sentence over with the name of one topping.

Five Little Pizzas

Cut five pizza shapes out of felt. Decorate them as described in the poem below, using felt scraps or felt-tip markers. Then place the shapes on a flannelboard and recite the poem.

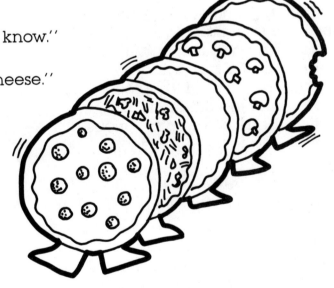

Five little pizzas all in a row.
The first one said,
"I'm made with pepperoni, you know."
The second one said,
"I'm made with sausage and cheese."
The third one said,
"Don't eat me, please."
The fourth one said,
"I'll be your dinner tonight."
The fifth one said,
"Someone has taken a bite!"
Five little pizzas all in a row.
Would you like to eat them?
Yes, I know!

Sue Schliecker
Waukesha, WI

I Wish I Were a Pepperoni Pizza

Sung to: "The Oscar Meyer
    Theme Song"

Oh, I wish I were a pepperoni pizza,
That is what I'd truly like to be.
For if I were a pepperoni pizza,
Everyone would be in love with me!

Let the children take turns naming their
favorite kinds of pizza and singing about
them.

Jean Warren

I Like Pizza

Sung to: "Skip to My Lou"

I like pizza, yes, I do.
I like pizza, yes, I do.
I like pizza, yes, I do.
And my tummy likes it, too!

*Naomi Lurey, Sharon Moscicki
Hoffman Estates, IL*

Pizza Puzzles

Cut out three cardboard circles
(approximately 12 inches in
diameter). Using felt-tip markers,
decorate the circles to resemble
pizzas. Cut one pizza in half, one
pizza in fourths and one pizza in
eighths. Place all of the pieces in a
pile and let the children take turns
putting them together in various
ways to make three pizzas.

Hint: For younger children, put out
the pieces for one pizza at a time.

Small, Medium and Large

Make three pizzas out of cardboard, one small, one medium-sized and one large. Talk about the differences in size. Then show the children three different sized objects such as a button, a block and a stuffed bear. Have the children compare the sizes of the three objects to determine which one is small, which one is medium-sized and which one is large. Then let them place the objects next to the matching sized pizzas.

Biscuit Pizzas

Prepare a variety of pizza toppings. Include tomato sauce and cheese plus any others the children would like (olives, mushrooms, onions, pepperoni, sausage, etc.). Give each child a refrigerator biscuit on a piece of foil that has his or her name on it. Have the children press their biscuits out from the centers to make mini pizza crusts. Then let them add their choice of toppings. Carefully lift the pizzas by the foil pieces and place them on a cookie sheet. Bake at 400 degrees for 10 minutes.

Extension: Turn this activity into a simple nutrition lesson by sorting the pizza ingredients into the four food groups (breads, fruits and vegetables, dairy products and meat products) and encouraging the children to use at least one ingredient from each group to make their pizzas.

Children's Books:
- *Cloudy With a Chance of Meatballs,* Judi Barrett, (Macmillan, 1978).
- *Curious George and the Pizza,* Margaret Rey, (Houghton Mifflin, 1985).

Contributors:
Judy Coiner, West Plains, MO
Sue Schliecker, Waukesha, WI

Popcorn Pictures

Let the children help make a batch of popcorn. Give each child a sheet of light blue construction paper and a large pan shape cut out of black construction paper. Have the children glue their pan shapes at the bottoms of their papers. Then let them glue pieces of popcorn "popping out of the pan" all over the rest of their papers.

Popcorn Wreaths

For each child cut out a cardboard wreath shape (about 7 inches across) and punch a hole in the top. Provide the children with glue and popped popcorn. Then have them glue the popcorn all over both sides of their wreaths. When the glue has dried, string ribbon or yarn through the holes in the tops of the wreaths to make hangers.

Variation: Let everyone help make one large wreath and give it to someone special.

Popcorn Matching

Number five index cards from 1 to 5. Glue from one to five pieces of popcorn on five more index cards. Let the children take turns counting the pieces of popcorn on the cards and matching them with the corresponding numbers.

Popcorn Snowfall

Put a clean white sheet on the floor. Place a hot air popcorn popper (with the top removed) in the center of the sheet and add popcorn kernels. Have the children sit around the edges of the sheet. Ask them what they think will happen when you turn on the popcorn popper. Can they guess why popcorn kernels pop? (When the kernels are heated, steam builds up inside of them until they burst.) Turn on the popcorn popper and watch as the corn pops and falls like snow.

Caution: Adults should always supervise activities that require electrical appliances.

Pop, Pop, Pop!

Have the children pretend to be popcorn kernels and crouch down on the floor. Choose a child to be "It" and have the child stand in the middle of the group with eyes closed. Silently signal one child to hide or leave the room. Then as "It" says "Popcorn, popcorn, pop, pop, pop!" have the other children begin hopping around and changing positions. When "It" says "Popcorn, popcorn, stop, stop, stop!" have the other children crouch back down and stay still. Then have "It" open his or her eyes and try to guess which child is hiding. If "It" guesses correctly, let the child who was hiding be the next "It." If not, let "It" choose another child who has not yet had a turn to take his or her place.

Creative Movement Fun

Ask the children to pretend that they are popcorn kernels inside a large popcorn popper. Have them lie on the floor and curl up into tiny balls. Tell them that you are going to turn on the heat and that gradually they will get hotter and hotter. Have them start squirming as they imagine the popper heating up. Eventually, have them get up on all fours and then into squatting positions. When they can't stand the heat any longer, have them pop up to become puffy popcorn pieces.

Popcorn Popping

Sung to: ''Old MacDonald
  Had a Farm''

Popcorn popping, oh, what fun!
Popping big and white.
We will wait until it's done,
Then we'll grab a bite.
With a pop, pop here,
And a pop, pop there,
Here a pop, there a pop,
Everywhere a pop, pop.
Popcorn popping, oh, what fun,
Popping big and white.

Elizabeth McKinnon

I'm a Little Kernel

Sung to: ''I'm a Little Teapot''

I'm a little kernel in a pot,
Turn on the heat and
  watch me hop.
When I get all warmed up,
  then I'll pop,
Umm, I taste good when I'm hot!

Neoma Kreuter
Ontario, CA

I Am Popcorn

Sung to: "Frere Jacques"

I am popcorn, I am popcorn.
In the pan, in the pan.
Watch me start hopping,
Watch me start popping.
Here I go — Pop! Pop! Pop!

Now I'm ready, now I'm ready.
Puffy and white, crunchy every bite.
Here comes the butter,
Here comes the salt.
Here I go — Now I'm gone!

Have the children act out the movements as they sing the song.

Aletha Ballengee
Fort Worth, TX

Flavored Popcorn

Let the children help make popcorn by measuring out the kernels. Explain that 1 tablespoon of kernels will make about 2 cups of popped corn. When the popcorn is done, flavor small amounts with parmesan cheese, taco seasoning and cinnamon for the children to sample. Then give each child some plain popcorn in a sandwich bag and let the child shake the popcorn with a pinch of the seasoning he or she likes best.

Children's Books:
- *Popcorn*, Frank Asch, (Crown, 1987).
- *Popcorn Book*, Tomie De Paola, (Holiday, 1978).

Contributors:
Cindy Davis, Finleyville, PA

Potato Prints

Cut brown paper bags into large potato shapes. Cut real potatoes into various small shapes. Place folded paper towels in shallow containers and pour on tempera paint. Then let the children dip the potato pieces into the paint and use them to print designs on their paper potato shapes.

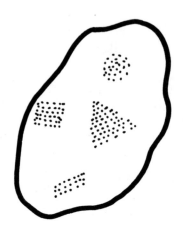

Potato Puppets

Give each child a potato shape cut out of brown construction paper. Have the children decorate their shapes with crayons or felt-tip markers. Let them add construction paper arms, if desired. Then attach Popsicle stick handles to the backs of their shapes to make potato puppets.

Sweet Potato Plants

Help the children each insert three or four toothpicks horizontally around the middle of a sweet potato. Have them balance the toothpicks on the rims of glass jars and add enough water to cover the bottom parts of their potatoes. Have them keep the water filled to this level. In about two weeks, vines will begin to sprout and the children will have sweet potato plants.

Five Little Potatoes

Read the following poem to the children. If desired, have them act out the movements while you read.

Five little potatoes
Growing in the ground,
Covered up with soft brown earth,
Making not a sound.

Down came the rain
One stormy summer day.
The five potatoes underground
Slept the day away.

Out came the sun.
The farmer came out, too.
Dug those five potatoes up
To give to me and you.

Mildred Hoffman
Tacoma, WA

Potato Game

Set out several different types of potatoes such as russet potatoes, red potatoes and sweet potatoes in various sizes. Let the children take turns sorting the potatoes by type. Then have them arrange the potatoes in each group from smallest to largest.

Potato Hop

Cut ten large potato shapes out of brown construction paper and number them from 1 to 10. Tape the shapes to the floor in the proper sequence. Then let the children take turns hopping from one potato to the other as everyone recites the rhyme below.

One potato, two potato,
Three potato, four,
Five potato, six potato,
Seven potato, more.
Eight potato, nine potato,
Here is ten.
Now let's start all over again.

Adapted Traditional

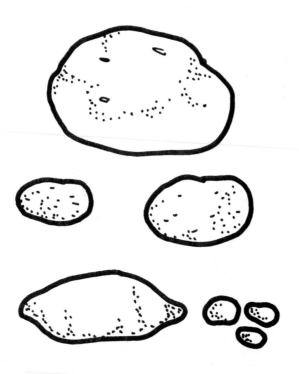

Mashed Potatoes

Cut cross sections of washed unpeeled potatoes about ¼ inch thick. Steam them in a steamer or an electric skillet for three minutes or until tender. When the potatoes have cooled, let the children help you mash them. Serve with butter, if desired.

Potato-Cheese Pancakes

Blend together 1 egg and 1 teaspoon milk. Let the children help grate one large potato and cheddar cheese to equal ¼ cup. Stir ingredients together in a bowl and add 1 tablespoon flour and salt and pepper to taste. Drop by spoonfuls into a hot greased frying pan. Cook until light brown on both sides.

Children's Books:
- *Potato Pancakes All Around,* Marilyn Hirsh, (Jewish Pub. Society, 1982).
- *Potatoes, Potatoes,* Anita Lobel, (Harper, 1984).
- *Potato,* Barrie Watt, (Silver Burdett, 1987).

Contributors:
Mildred Hoffman, Tacoma, WA
Joyce Marshall, Whitby, Ontario

Pumpkin Printing

After Halloween, use your carved jack-o'-lantern for print making. Cut the pumpkin into chunks and let the children use nails to carve designs on the insides of the pumpkin pieces. Then have them press the design sides of their pumpkin pieces first on ink pads and then on pieces of construction paper.

Pumpkin Pies

Cut round pie shapes out of orange construction paper. Set out small containers of powdered cinnamon and ginger and place a few whole cloves in a paper cup for each child. Have the children brush glue on their pie shapes. Then let them sprinkle the spices over the glue to create fragrant ''pumpkin pies.''

Pumpkin Patch

Have the children fill paper lunch sacks with small pieces of crumpled newspaper. Secure each bag with a twist tie, leaving about 1 inch of the bag gathered at the top. Then have the children paint the bottom parts of their bags orange and the gathered parts green to create pumpkins with stems. When the pumpkins have dried, string them all together with green yarn ''vines'' to make a ''pumpkin patch.''

Pumpkin Discrimination

Make six pairs of pumpkin faces on twelve white index cards. Mix up the cards. Let the children take turns matching the pumpkin faces. If desired, start with only four cards (two pairs) and increase the number of pairs as the children's discrimination abilities increase.

Personalized Pumpkins

If you have room for a garden, let the children grow personalized pumpkins. When the pumpkins are small and green (about the size of grapefruit) help the children scratch their names on the outsides with a nail or a small knife. As the pumpkins grow, scars will form over the scratches and the names will get bigger.

Pumpkin Growth

On four large index cards draw the growth stages of a pumpkin (a seed, a flowering vine, a green pumpkin and a ripe pumpkin). Mix up the cards and let the children take turns putting them in order.

Ten Little Pumpkins

Cut ten pumpkin shapes out of orange felt and place them on a flannelboard. Remove the shapes one at a time as you read the following poem.

Ten little pumpkins
All in a line,
One became a jack-o'-lantern,
Then there were nine.

Nine little pumpkins
Peeking through the gate,
An old witch took one,
Then there were eight.

Eight little pumpkins
(There never were eleven),
A green goblin took one,
Then there were seven.

Seven little pumpkins
Full of jolly tricks,
A white ghost took one,
Then there were six.

Six little pumpkins
Glad to be alive,
A black cat took one,
Then there were five.

Five little pumpkins
By the barn door,
A hoot owl took one,
Then there were four.

Four little pumpkins
(As you can plainly see),
One became a pumpkin pie,
Then there were three.

Three little pumpkins
Feeling very blue,
One rolled far away,
Then there were two.

Two little pumpkins
Alone in the sun,
One said, "So long,"
And then there was one.

One little pumpkin
Left all alone,
A little boy chose him,
Then there were none.

Ten little pumpkins
In a patch so green
Made everyone happy
On Halloween.

Author Unknown

Jack-O'-Lantern Flashlights

Out of orange construction paper cut circles to cover the ends of several flashlights. Cut jack-o'-lantern facial features out of each circle. Tape the circles to the ends of the flashlights. Give the children the flashlights and let them dance around a darkened room, shining their jack-o'-lantern faces all around.

Mr. Pumpkin
Sung to: "Frere Jacques"

Mr. Pumpkin, Mr. Pumpkin,
Eyes so round, eyes so round.
Halloween is coming,
Halloween is coming,
To my town, to my town.

*Susan M. Paprocki
Northbrook, IL*

Banana-Pumpkin Foamy

Blend 1 cup milk, 1 sliced banana, 2 tablespoons canned pumpkin and a dash of cinnamon together for a foamy pumpkin drink. Makes 2 servings.

Orange Pumpkin Pudding

Dice 4 pieces of whole-wheat bread and crumble them in a blender. Place the crumbs in a large bowl. Next, blend together ½ cup milk, ½ cup orange juice and ¼ cup unsweetened frozen apple juice concentrate. Add 2 eggs, 1 sliced banana, 2 teaspoons cinnamon, 1 cup cooked pumpkin and a dash of salt and blend again. Add the mixture to the bread crumbs. Stir together and pour into a baking dish. Bake for 50 minutes at 350 degrees. Serve slightly warm and top with whipped cream, if desired. Makes 8 servings.

Children's Books:
- *Mousekin's Golden House*, Edna Miller, (Prentice Hall, 1964).
- *Pumpkin Pumpkin*, Jeanne Titherington, (Greenwillow, 1986).
- *Vanishing Pumpkin*, Tony Johnston, (Putnam, 1983).

Contributors:
Barbara Fletcher, El Cajon, CA
Cathy Griffin, Princeton, NJ
Betty Silkunas, Lansdale, PA

Rain Painting

On a rainy day give each child a paper plate. Let the children sprinkle a few drops of food coloring (or shake a little powdered tempera) on their plates. Have them put on their raincoats and walk outside, holding their plates in the rain for about a minute. After they bring their plates inside, talk about the designs created by the rain.

Umbrellas

Let the children paint large umbrella shapes cut out of butcher paper. Hang the umbrella paintings on a wall or a bulletin board and attach cane-shaped handles.

Making Rain

Boil some water in a pot (or a tea kettle) until steam forms above it. Then fill a pie pan with ice cubes and hold it above the pot in the steam "cloud." Have the children observe that when the steam comes in contact with the cool air from the pie pan, drops of water form and fall back into the pot like rain.

Caution: Adults should always supervise activities that require electrical appliances.

Rain Book

Staple together four to six pieces of white paper to make a book for each child. Write the words "Rain Helps Things Grow" on the cover of each book. Let the children look through magazines and tear out pictures of things that need rain to help them grow such as trees, flowers and other plants. Then have the children glue the pictures in their books.

Rainy Day Nursery Rhymes

Rain on the green grass,
    (Flutter fingers down to ground.)
And rain on the tree.
    (Flutter fingers up over head.)
Rain on the housetop,
    (Make upside-down "V" with hands and arms.)
But not on me.
    (Circle arms over head to make "umbrella.")

Read the poem again and let the children take turns filling in the blanks.

Rain on the _____,
And rain on the tree.
Rain on the _____,
But not on me.

Adapted Traditional

Rain, rain, go to Spain.
    (Push away with hands.)
Never show your face again.
    (Cover face with hands.)

Traditional

Rain, rain, go away,
Come again another day,
Little (child's name)
Wants to play.

Let the child named tell what he or she wants to play.

Traditional

Counting Raindrops

Cut five umbrella shapes and fifteen raindrop shapes out of felt. Number the umbrella shapes from 1 to 5 and place them on a flannelboard. Let the children take turns identifying the number on each umbrella and placing the corresponding number of raindrops above it.

Puddle Jumping

Place several carpet squares around the room. Have the children pretend that the squares are puddles. Let them practice jumping into and over the puddles.

RAIN

Eensy, Weensy Raindrops
Sung to: "Eensy, Weensy Spider"

Some eensy, weensy raindrops
Are falling from the sky.
They're filling up the puddles
And dropping in my eye.
Drip, drip and drop, drop,
I love to hear them fall,
For the eensy, weensy raindrops
Mean wet fun for us all.

Betty Silkunas
Lansdale, PA

Rain, Rain Falling Down
Sung to: "Row, Row, Row Your Boat"

Rain, rain falling down,
    (Wiggle fingers downward.)
Falling on the ground.
Pitter, patter, pitter, patter,
What a lovely sound.

Susan A. Miller
Kutztown, PA

It Is Raining
Sung to: "Frere Jacques"

It is raining, it is raining,
On my head, on my head.
Pitter, patter raindrops,
Pitter, patter raindrops.
I'm all wet! I'm all wet!

Susan Widdifield
Poulsbo, WA

Rain

Sung to: "Row, Row, Row Your Boat"

Rain, rain falling down,
> (Flutter fingers up and down.)

Landing all around.
> (Move arms out to sides.)

What a lovely sound you make
> (Cup hands behind ears.)

Splashing on the ground.
> (Wiggle fingers up and down.)

Rain, rain tumbling down,
> (Lower hands while circling them
> around each other.)

Crashing to the ground.
> (Quickly crouch down and huddle on floor.)

What a scary noise you make
> (Cover ears.)

As you tumble down.
> (Huddle down lower.)

Use this song to teach the concepts of soft
and loud by singing the first verse in a soft
voice and the second verse in a loud
voice.

Susan L. Moon
Allentown, PA

Children's Books:
- *Mushroom in the Rain*, Mirra Ginsburg,
  (Macmillan, 1974).
- *Rain*, Peter Spier, (Doubleday, 1982).
- *Tattie's River Journey*, Shirley Murphy,
  (Dial, 1983).

Reindeer Faces

Give each child a piece of brown or yellow construction paper. Help the children trace around both their hands on their papers. Have them cut out their hand shapes and set them aside to use for antlers. Give the children large brown construction paper triangles to use for reindeer faces. Have them place their triangles, points down, on a table. Help them fold over the two upper corners of their triangles to make ears. Then have them glue their hand-shaped antlers at the tops of their triangles and add black construction paper circles for eyes and noses.

Antler Painting

Set out small tree branches, shallow pans of tempera paint and large pieces of construction paper. Let the children pretend that the branches are antlers. Have them dip the tips of the antlers into the paint, then gently brush them across their papers.

Reindeer Puppets

Give the children triangles cut out of brown posterboard to use for reindeer faces. Help them each tape two twigs to the backs of their triangles for antlers. Then let them glue on black construction paper circles for eyes and noses. Complete the puppets by attaching Popsicle stick handles to the backs of the reindeer faces.

Running Reindeer

Discuss the many different ways that people and animals can run. Have the children pretend to be reindeer. Ask them to experiment with different ways of running such as fast, slow, backward, in slow motion, in place, in a circle, on tip-toes, side-by-side with a partner, in a race with giant strides or through the snow with prancing steps.

Reindeer Tracks

Discuss with the children the kinds of tracks different animals make. Show them pictures of reindeer and other animal tracks. Talk about how tracks are made in snow or mud.

Extension: Cut sponge pieces into reindeer track shapes and glue them on small pieces of wood. Let the children make their own reindeer tracks by pressing the sponge stamps first on ink pads, then on pieces of construction paper.

Track Matching

Draw matching pictures of different animal tracks (including reindeer tracks) on pairs of index cards. Then mix up the cards and let the children take turns finding the matching pairs of tracks.

Variation: For a more difficult game, draw pictures of animals on one set of index cards and pictures of their tracks on another set. Then have the children match each animal to its tracks.

Ten Little Reindeer
Sung to: "Ten Little Indians"

One little, two little,
Three little reindeer,
Four little, five little,
Six little reindeer,
Seven little, eight little,
Nine little reindeer,
Playing in the snow.

Judith McNitt
Adrian, MI

Reindeer Sandwiches

To make 4 reindeer sandwiches, you will need 1 slice of bread, 8 celery sticks, peanut butter, 8 raisins and 4 cherries or red berries. The night before, remove the crust from the slice of bread and cut it twice diagonally to make 4 triangular pieces. Freeze the cut pieces of bread. (It is easier for children to spread peanut butter on frozen bread.) Slice each of the celery sticks halfway down and refrigerate them overnight in a bowl of water. (The sliced halves of the celery sticks will curl outward

and resemble antlers.) The next day have the children spread peanut butter on their frozen bread triangles and place them points down on small plates. Then let them create reindeer faces by adding raisins for eyes, cherries for noses and celery sticks for antlers.

Children's Books:
Polar Express, Chris Van Allsburg, (Houghton Mifflin, 1985).
Rudolph the Red Nosed Reindeer, Barbara Hazen, (Western, 1985).

Contributors:
Vicki Claybrook, Kennewick, WA
Barb Mazzochi, Villa Park, IL
Sharon L. Olson, Minot, ND

Rock Sculptures

Set out a variety of small rocks, glue and squares of cardboard. Let the children glue the rocks on the cardboard squares to create rock sculptures.

Painting Rocks

Have the children collect medium-sized rocks. Let them paint designs on their rocks with tempera paint. If desired, give them bits of yarn, rickrack and buttons to glue on their rocks to add special details.

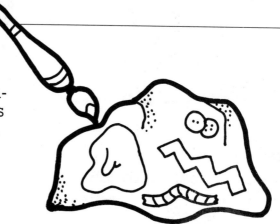

Gravelly Designs

Fill a large shallow box with pea gravel. Let the children take turns making designs in the gravel with tongue depressors or with their fingers.

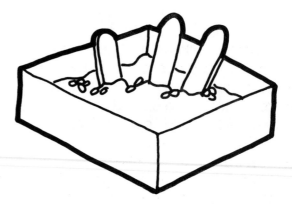

Rock Collections

If you live in an area where there are different varieties of rocks, take the children on a rock gathering expedition. Let the children have fun sorting their rocks by size, color, markings, etc. Have them try washing their rocks and examining them with magnifying glasses. Or have them try scraping their rocks with nails to see if they are hard or soft.

Rock Stories

Have each child collect four or five rocks and play "house" with them. Encourage the children to tell you about each person in their pretend rock families. For example, they could tell you the names of their rocks and what each rock likes to do. Help them to expand their stories as much as possible by asking questions.

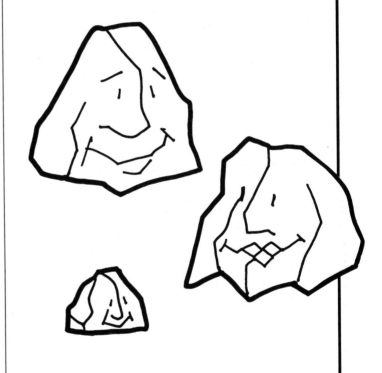

ROCKS

Indian Counting Game

Let the children play this version of an Indian counting game. Assemble five smooth pebbles. Paint a half-moon shape on one side of each of four pebbles and a star shape on one side of the remaining pebble. Place the pebbles in a shallow basket or wooden bowl. Let one child at a time hold the basket and give it a shake. Then have the child count the number of shapes that turn up, allotting one point for each moon and two points for the star. The child who has the highest number of points at the end of the game wins.

Rock Sorter

Make a rock sorter by cutting four or five holes from large to small in the top of a shoe box. Give the children a number of different sized rocks. Then let them sort their rocks in the rock sorter by placing each rock in the hole closest to its size.

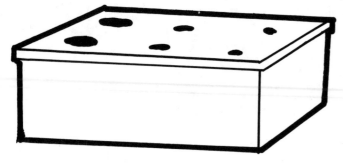

Making Stone Soup Today
Sung to: "The Paw Paw Patch"

Pick up a stone and
Put it in the pot,
Pick up a stone and
Put it in the pot.
Pick up a stone and
Put it in the pot,
Making stone soup today.

Continue, letting the children name other ingredients for the soup.

Jean Warren

Stone Soup

Read or tell the folktale "Stone Soup" before starting this activity. Fill a pot with 2 quarts water. Add chopped carrots, celery, turnips, potatoes, onions, zucchini, tomatoes and a smooth round rock that has been scrubbed and boiled. Bring the water in the pot to a boil, then simmer for 1 hour. When the vegetables are tender, add stock or bouillon and season to taste. If desired, add small pieces of cooked meat or chicken shortly before serving.

Children's Books:
- *Everybody Needs a Rock*, Byrd Baylor, (Macmillan, 1974).
- *Sylvester and the Magic Pebble*, William Steig, (Prentice Hall, 1969).

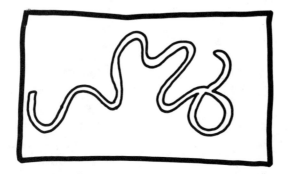

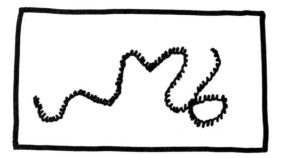

Sand Pictures

Let the children use glue to paint pictures or designs on sheets of construction paper. Then have them sprinkle pinches of sand over the glue. Have them wait a few moments before shaking off the excess.

Variation: Color the sand first by mixing it with small amounts of powdered tempera paint. Then pour the sand into shaker containers.

Sand Dough

Add sand to playdough for a different kind of texture experience. Encourage the children to describe how the playdough feels as they work with it. Playdough can be made by mixing together 2 cups flour, 1 cup salt, 1 cup water and a few drops of oil or liquid detergent.

What Is Sand?

Talk about sand with the children. What is sand? Where does it come from? How is it made? Set out sand, rocks, shells and magnifying glasses. Explain to the children that powerful waves smash rocks and shells into tiny pieces which we call "sand." Then let the children use the magnifying glasses to explore the similarities and differences between the sand, the rocks and the shells.

Sand Play

Let the children take turns playing in dishpans of sand. Give them different kinds of utensils to experiment with, such as measuring cups, small plastic containers, molds, scoops, sifters and sand combs. For variety, add water to some of the dishpans. Let the children try using cookie cutters in the wet sand.

Sand Writing

Place a tray of sand in front of the children. With your finger, write an alphabet letter in the sand. Ask the children to identify the letter. When they have done so, smooth out the sand and write another letter. Follow the same procedure for reviewing numbers and shapes. Then let the children take turns writing letters, numbers and shapes in the sand themselves.

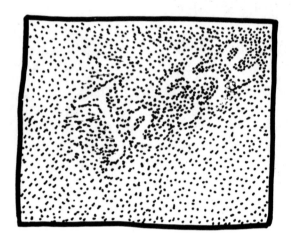

At the Beach

Have the children act out the movements as they recite the poem below.

I dig holes in the sand with my fingers.
  (Wiggle fingers.)
I dig holes in the sand with my toes.
  (Wiggle toes.)
Then I pour some water in the holes —
  (Pretend to pour water.)
I wonder where it goes.
  (Move hands out to sides, palms up.)

Elizabeth McKinnon

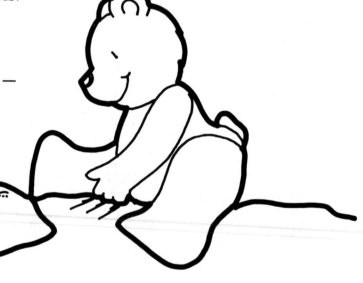

Buried Treasure

Fill a box with sand and hide five small objects in it, such as a shell, a pebble, a crayon, a bead and a button. Let the children search for the ''buried treasure,'' one or two at a time. When they have found as many of the treasures as they can, ask them to count the objects or to match them to cards with pictures of the hidden objects drawn on them. Provide a sifter for the children to use when searching for the treasure, if desired.

Variation: Hide plastic letters in the sand. Each time the children find one, have them name words that begin with that letter.

Sandbox Song
Sung to: ''Frere Jacques''

Make a sand cake,
Make a castle
In the sand,
In the sand.
Pouring, measuring, digging,
Pouring, measuring, digging
Just feels grand,
Just feels grand.

Betty Silkunas
Lansdale, PA

Sand
Sung to: ''Frere Jacques''

Sand is gritty,
Sand is gritty,
At the beach,
At the beach.
Sand is many tiny rocks
Broken down from bigger rocks,
At the beach,
At the beach.

Susan Peters
Upland, CA

Children's Books:
- *Quicksand Book*, Tomie De Paola, (Holiday, 1977).
- *Sand Cake*, Frank Asch, (Crown, 1987).
- *The Sun, the Wind and the Rain*, Lisa Peters, (Henry Holt, 1988).

Contributors:
Susan Peters, Upland, CA
Dawn Picollelli, Wilmington, DE
Betty Silkunas, Lansdale, PA

SHADOWS

Shadow Pictures

Let each child take a sheet of white construction paper to an outside area. Have the children hold their papers behind leaves or grass to create shadow pictures with the help of the sun. As the pictures last only a moment, have the children work in pairs and share shadow creations with their partners.

Shadow Line-Up

Have the children go outside on a sunny day. Line them up and see if they can identify their shadows. Ask questions such as these:

"Can you spot your own shadow? How can you tell it is yours? What causes shadows?"

Shadow Puppets

Cut people or animal shapes out of posterboard. Attach the shapes to tongue depressors. Shine a light on a wall and let the children move their puppets in front of the light. Show them how to make small shadows by standing close to the wall and large shadows by standing far back. Then let them use their shadow puppets to act out the movements described in the poem below.

There is a little shadow
That dances on my wall.
Sometimes it's big and scary,
Sometimes it's very small.

Sometimes it's oh, so quiet
And doesn't move at all.
Then other times it chases me
Or bounces like a ball.

I'd love to meet that shadow
Who dances in the night,
But it always runs away
In the morning light.

Jean Warren

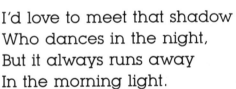

Shadow Poem

Write the initial letters of the lines in the poem below on separate squares of paper. Back the squares with felt strips. Then place the letters on a flannelboard to spell ''shadow'' as you read the poem to the children.

S un is shining, let's go for a walk,
H urry outside and around the block.
A t your side walks a little friend, too,
D oes the very same things you do.
O pen the door and go inside —
W here, oh, where does my shadow friend hide?

Mildred Hoffman
Tacoma, WA

Shadow Partners

Divide the children into pairs. Have the children in each pair face one another. Ask one child in each pair to move his or her hands slowly while the other child shadows his or her movements. Then have the children reverse roles.

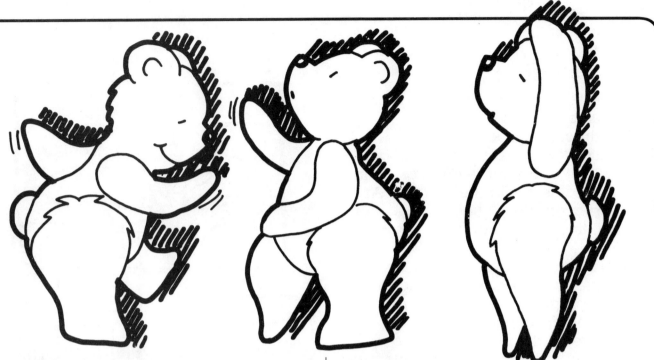

Shadow Dancing

Arrange a bright light to shine on you so that it casts your shadow on a wall. Show the children what a clever shadow you have and how it does everything you do. Show them how you can make your shadow wave, dance, twirl and even fall down. Then let the children take turns performing with their own shadows while everyone sings the song on this page.

Shadow Song

Sung to: "Skip to My Lou"

Dance, dance, just like me,
Dance, dance, just like me.
Dance, dance, just like me,
Little shadow, just like me.

Additional verses: "Raise your hand, just like me; Kick your foot, just like me; Bend way down, just like me; Flap your arms, just like me."

Jean Warren

Children's Books:
• *Bear Shadow*, Frank Asch, (Prentice Hall, 1985).
• *Shadows*, Taro Gomi, (Heian, 1981).

Contributors:
Mildred Hoffman, Tacoma, WA

Frosty Pictures

Have the children draw outdoor pictures on pieces of colored construction paper. Make a solution of half Epsom salts and half water. Have the children paint their pictures with the mixture. As the mixture dries, it will leave sparkling crystals on their papers.

Variation: Turn greeting card pictures into snow scenes. Have the children paint over the pictures with the Epsom salts and water mixture. Or let them brush the pictures with glue and sprinkle on glitter.

Simple Snowflakes

Show the children how to fold coffee filters in half and then in half again. Have them cut small triangles out of the folded edges. Then have them unfold their filters to see the snowflakes they have created.

Q-Tip Snowflakes

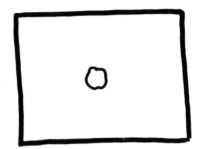  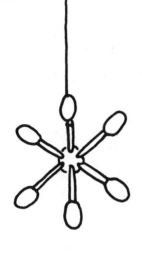

Give each child three Q-Tips cut in half and a small square of aluminum foil. Squeeze a small amount of glue in the center of each piece of foil. Have the children arrange their six Q-Tip pieces on their foil squares with the cut ends of the Q-Tips touching to make star-like snowflakes. When the glue completely dries, peel off the foil pieces. Then tie loops of thread to the snowflakes and hang them in a window.

Snowballs

Let the children go outside and make two small snowballs. Have them place each snowball in a paper cup. Place one cup outside and one cup inside. Together, observe the two snowballs. Ask the children to tell you what is happening to the snow. Why is the snow melting inside but not outside?

SNOW

Snowflakes

Catch snowflakes on a piece of black construction paper. Let the children examine the snowflakes with a magnifying glass. Explain that snowflakes are frozen water crystals and that each flake is unique with its own design.

Snow Pal Puppets

Cut snow pal shapes out of small white index cards. Cut two finger holes at the bottom of each shape. Show the children how to make legs for their puppets by sticking two fingers through the holes. Recite the following poem with the children and have them act out the movements with their puppets. Then repeat the poem, letting the children name other movements for their snow pal puppets to act out.

Snow pal, Snow pal,
Running down the street,
Watch what it does
With its snow pal feet.

Jean Warren

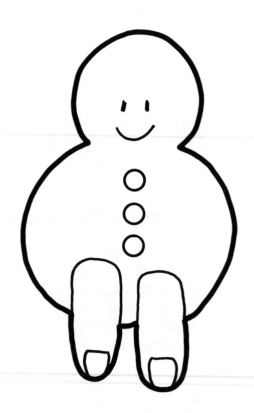

Circle Snow Pals

For each child cut a large, a medium-sized and a small circle out of white construction paper. Mix up the circles and have the children sort them by size into three piles. Then let them each take a large circle and place it on a table. Next, have them each put a medium-sized circle above the large one. Finally, have them each put a small circle above the medium-sized one. Then give each child a small black top hat shape to put on top of his or her circle snow pal.

Snow Pals

Have the children lie on the floor and stretch out to form a beautiful blanket of snow. Next, have them pretend that boys and girls are rolling them up to make large snowballs. Let the children roll across the floor, finally becoming so large they have to stand up and become snow pals.

What a Pretty Sight
Sung to: "Row, Row, Row Your Boat"

Snow, snow swirling round,
> (Move hands in circular motions.)

Falling to the ground.
> (Kneel and continue hand motions.)

What a pretty sight you make,
> (Cup hands over eyes and look right and left.)

Dancing all around.
> (Turn and dance in circles.)

Snow, snow swirling round,
> (Move hands in circular motions.)

Flying through the air.
> (Wave arms.)

What a pretty sight you make,
> (Cup hands over eyes and look right and left.)

Dancing everywhere.
> (Turn and dance in circles.)

Susan L. Moon
Allentown, PA

Sing a Song of Winter
Sung to: "Sing a Song of Sixpence"

Sing a song of winter,
Frost is in the air.
Sing a song of winter,
Snowflakes everywhere.
Sing a song of winter,
Hear the sleighbells chime.
Can you think of anything
As nice as wintertime?

Judith McNitt
Adrian, MI

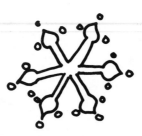

Snowflakes Falling

Sung to: "Mary Had a Little Lamb"

Snowflakes falling
From the sky,
From the sky,
From the sky.
Snowflakes falling
From the sky
To the earth below.

Watch them as they
Dance and whirl,
Dance and whirl,
Dance and whirl.
Watch them as they
Dance and whirl,
Soft white winter snow.

Judith McNitt
Adrian, MI

Children's Books:
- *Snowman*, Raymond Briggs, (Random, 1986).
- *Snowy Day*, Ezra Jack Keats, (Viking, 1962).
- *Owl Moon*, Jane Yolen, (Putnam, 1987).

Dance Around the Snow Pal

Sung to: "The Mulberry Bush"

This is the way
We dance around,
Dance around, dance around,
This is the way
We dance around
Our snow pal in the morning.

This is the way
We skip around,
Skip around, skip around,
This is the way
We skip around
Our snow pal in the morning.

This is the way
We twirl around,
Twirl around, twirl around,
This is the way
We twirl around
Our snow pal in the morning.

Jean Warren

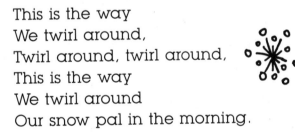

Contributors:
Betty Silkunas, Lansdale, PA

Making Spider Webs

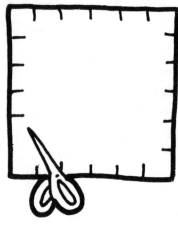 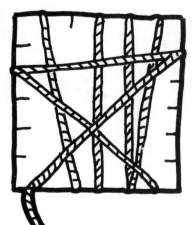

Cut squares out of white poster-board and make slits around the edges. Tape a piece of black yarn to the back of each square and pull it through one of the slits. Then have the children cross the yarn back and forth over the fronts of their squares, attaching it through the slits (slits can be used more than once). Trim the ends of the yarn and tape them to the backs of the squares.

Variation: Use black thread instead of yarn.

Egg Cup Spiders

Give each child a cardboard egg carton cup and four 4-inch pipe cleaner pieces. Help the children poke their pipe cleaners through their egg cups to make spider legs. Have them bend the legs slightly downward. Let the children paint their spiders black and glue on plastic moving eyes, if desired.

Spider Webs

Discuss spiders and their webs with the children. Show pictures from books of different types of spider webs. Go on a nature walk to look for spider webs. (Morning walks are best for spotting webs because they glisten with dew.) Bring a web inside for the children to observe. To capture the web, spray a piece of black construction paper with hairspray, then move the paper up behind the web until it adheres to the sticky surface.

Web Making

Have eight or more children sit on the floor in a circle. Give a ball of yarn to one child. Have the child hold onto the loose end of the yarn and roll the ball to another child. Have that child grasp hold of the loose yarn and roll the ball to a third child. Let the children continue rolling the ball back and forth until everyone is holding onto the yarn. Then stop the game and let the children admire the web they have created.

One Spider Went Out to Play

Have the children sit at random on the floor. Recite the following verse as you walk among them.

One spider went out to play,
Out on a spider's web one day.
He had such enormous fun,
He called for another spider to come.

At the end of the verse, choose one child to hook onto your "spider train." Repeat the verse, this time saying "Two spiders went out to play," and choose another child to join the fun. Continue the game until the children have formed one long spider train. Then recite the final verse below and have the children act out the movements described.

All the spiders went out to play,
Out on a spider's web one day.
They had such enormous fun,
They didn't see the web break —
    (Clap hands.)
And they all fell down!

Adapted Traditional

Spin, Spin Little Spider

Sung to: "Ten Little Indians"

Spin, spin, little spider,
Spin, spin, wider, wider.
Spin, spin, little spider,
Early in the morning.

Dance, dance, little spider,
Dance, dance, dance out wider.
Dance, dance, little spider,
Early in the morning.

Make your web, little spider,
Make your web, wider, wider.
Make your web, little spider,
Early in the morning.

Jean Warren

Prune Spiders

Give each of the children a large soft prune to use as a spider body. Then let them poke pretzel sticks or crispy Chinese noodles into the sides of their prunes to make legs.

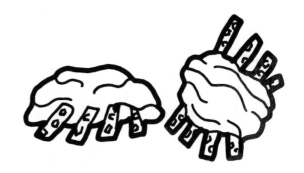

Children's Books:
- *The Big Sneeze*, Ruth Brown, (Lothrop, 1985).
- *Spider's Web*, Barrie Watts, (Silver Burdett, 1987).
- *The Very Busy Spider*, Eric Carle, (Putnam, 1984).

Contributors:
Mary Whaley, Kentland, IN
Peggy Wolf, Pittsburgh, PA

To Make a Star

Fold a rectangular piece of paper in half. Then with the folded edge at the bottom, fold the paper as indicated by the arrows and dotted lines in the illustration below. Cut through all thicknesses as shown.

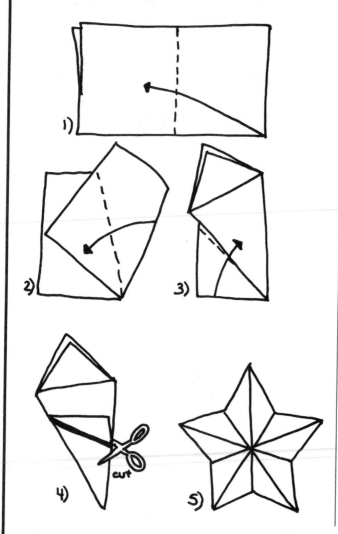

You're a Star

Let the children be the stars of a bulletin board display you make together. Cut stars out of construction paper, one for each child. Have the children draw pictures of themselves on the stars. Then attach the stars to a bulletin board and add the title 'You're a Star.'

Variation: Glue a photograph of each child on a star cut out of foil. Then pin the stars on a bulletin board.

Shining Stars

Have the children dip star-shaped cookie cutters (or potatoes cut into star shapes) into paint and press them on paper to make prints. Let them sprinkle glitter on the wet paint to make shining stars.

Nighttime Surprises

For each child use a white crayon to draw stars on a piece of white construction paper. (Press down hard with the crayon while drawing.) Set out the papers along with brushes and black tempera thinned with water to make a wash. Then let the children brush the tempera wash over their papers to discover the star surprises that will show through.

Star Scopes

Give each child an empty toilet tissue tube with a black paper circle taped over one end. Let the children gently punch holes in the paper-covered ends of their tubes with toothpicks to complete their star scopes. To use, have the children hold their scopes up to the light and look through the uncovered ends. The light will shine through the holes, creating miniature planetariums.

Star Experiment

Ask the children why they think they can see stars only at night. Then ask them to help you do this experiment. Turn on all the lights in your room. Have two or three children stand away from the group and give them each a flashlight that has been turned on. Ask the group if they can see the light from the flashlights. Gradually darken the room. What happens to the light coming from the flashlights? Does it become easier or harder to see? Help the children to understand that just as they can't see the light from the flashlights when the room lights are on, they can't see the light from the stars when the sun is shining.

Color Stars

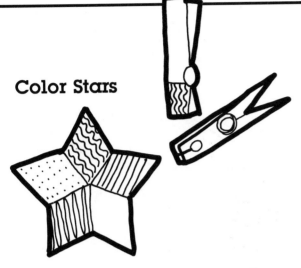

Make a matching game for the children by cutting a star out of cardboard and coloring each of its five points a different color. Then color the ends of five clothespins to match the colors on the star points. To play the game, have the children clip the clothespins on the matching colored star points.

Arranging Stars

Cut out several sizes of stars. Let the children arrange them in order from smallest to largest. Then have them count the stars.

Star Folders

Draw eight stars on the insides of a file folder and number them from 1 to 8. Draw matching stars on construction paper or index cards and cut them out. Use dots to number the stars from 1 to 8. Give the children the file folder and the cutout stars. Let them take turns matching the numbers by placing the cutouts on the corresponding pictures on the file folder.

STARS

Wish Upon a Star

Cut a star out of cardboard and cover it with foil. Tell the children that it is a special wishing star and that whoever holds it gets to make a wish. Then give the star to one child and let him or her make a wish. Pass the star around the group until everyone has had a turn making a wish.

Twinkle, Twinkle, Little Stars
Sung to: ``Music, Music, Music''

Twinkle, twinkle, little stars,
Friends of Jupiter and Mars,
All you do the whole night through
Is twinkle, twinkle, twinkle.
Shine, oh, friends of mine,
If wishes really, really do come true,
I will wish tonight on you.
Please, oh please, oh please come true,
The wish I wish tonight on you,
Then tomorrow all day through
I'll twinkle, twinkle, twinkle.

Jean Warren

The Stars Are Shining Bright
Sung to: "The Farmer in the Dell"

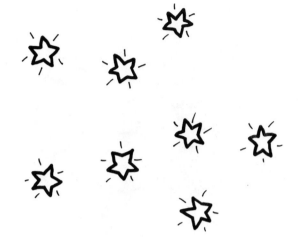

The stars are shining bright,
See their twinkling light.
When you see the sky at night,
The stars are shining bright.

Gayle Bittinger

Star Cookies

Use a favorite recipe to make sugar cookies. Let the children roll out the dough and use star-shaped cookie cutters to cut out star cookies. Arrange the cookies on a cookie sheet and let the children sprinkle them with colored sugar crystals before baking.

Star Sandwiches

Let the children use star-shaped cookie cutters to cut stars out of pieces of bread. Have them spread softened cream cheese on their stars before eating.

Children's Books:
- *Dawn*, Uri Shulevitz, (Farrar, Straus & Giroux, 1974).
- *Sky Is Full of Stars*, Franklyn Branley, (Harper Row, 1983).
- *Watch the Stars Come Out*, Riki Levinson, (Macmillan, 1985).

Sunny Faces

Tape white construction paper circles to a tabletop. Let the children paint the circles yellow. When the paint has dried, untape the circles and help the children draw on happy faces with felt-tip markers. Then have the children glue short yellow streamers around the edges of their sunny faces.

Sun Puppets

For each child cut two small circles out of yellow construction paper. Help each child glue his or her circles together with a Popsicle stick handle in between. Then let the children glue short pieces of yellow yarn around the edges of their circles to make sun rays.

Paint Blob Suns

Give each child a piece of white construction paper and a Q-Tip. Place a blob of yellow paint in the center of each paper. Have the children use their Q-Tips to draw the paint out from the blobs in long rays to create suns.

Plant Experiment

Set out two identical plants. Help the children place one plant in a dark closet and the other on a sunny windowsill. Water the plants as needed. Check the plants every day and have the children observe the differences between them. Which plant is healthier? Why?

Sun Prints

Have the children place objects such as erasers, pencils or blocks on pieces of dark colored construction paper. Set the papers in direct sunlight. At the end of the day, have the children remove the objects and observe what has happened to the paper. Which spots are lighter than others? Why?

Sunshine Everywhere

Recite the poem below with the children, letting them take turns filling in the blanks.

The morning sun peeked through the trees
To kiss the _____ and the honey bees.
It danced by the _____ and the fields of hay
Until it reached the _____ where it stayed all day.
Sun, sun, don't you run.
Stay with me and have some fun.
Shine on the _____, shine on me.
Shine on the _____, shine on the tree.
Shine on the _____, shine so fair.
Shine on the _____, shine everywhere!

Jean Warren

Suns in the Sky

Have the children stand about 3 feet apart and give them each a yellow balloon "sun." Have them bat their balloon suns up into the air and try keeping them up without moving from their spaces. When a balloon falls outside of a child's space or reach, have the child sit down. Continue the game until no one is standing.

Sing a Song of Sunshine

Sung to: "Sing a Song of Sixpence"

Sing a song of sunshine,
Be happy every day.
Sing a song of sunshine,
You'll chase the clouds away.
Be happy every moment,
No matter what you do.
Just sing and sing and sing and sing,
And let the sunshine through!

Jean Warren

Sunshine Shake

In a blender combine one 6-ounce can unsweetened frozen orange juice concentrate, ¾ cup milk, ¾ cup water, 1 teaspoon vanilla and 6 ice cubes. Makes 4 servings.

Children's Books:
- *Arrow to the Sun*, Gerald McDermott, (Viking, 1974).
- *Sun Up, Sun Down*, Gail Gibbons, (Harcourt, 1983).
- *The Way to Start a Day*, Byrd Baylor, (Macmillan, 1978).

Contributors:
Kay Roozen, Des Moines, IA
Saundra Winnett, Lewisville, TX

Smiling Pictures

Give each child a 6- by 4-inch pair of smiling lips cut out of red construction paper and an 8- by ½-inch strip of white paper. Have the children snip off little pieces of their white paper strips to make "teeth." Then let them glue their paper teeth on their paper lips to make big toothy smiles.

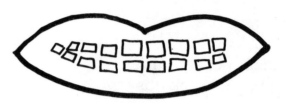

Toothbrush Painting

Cut a large tooth shape out of white construction paper for each child. Have the children dip old toothbrushes into white tempera paint "toothpaste" and then use them to "brush" their paper teeth. Show the children how to brush up and down, back and forth and in a circular motion.

Hint: This is excellent practice for the real thing, but be sure to stress that the brushes and the pretend toothpaste should not be put into real mouths.

Toothy Puppets

Have each child draw a face on the top part of a folded paper plate. Then give the children bits of Styrofoam to glue inside their plates for "teeth." To work their puppets, have the children hold them with both hands. Then let them open and close their puppets' tooth-filled mouths to make them "talk."

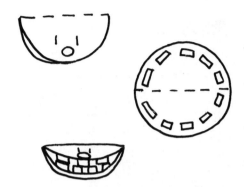

Caution: Use this activity with older children who will not be tempted to put the pretend teeth into their own mouths. Styrofoam bits contain chemicals that may be toxic if swallowed.

Tile Teeth

Fill several small containers with foods that will stain or stick to teeth, such as ketchup, grape juice and syrup. Place the containers on a table along with Q-Tips, small white ceramic tiles, old toothbrushes, toothpaste and two or three glasses of water. Let the children use the Q-Tips to spread small amounts of the foods on the ceramic tile "teeth." After the foods have dried, let the children remove them from their tiles by using the tooth-brushes and toothpaste. Encourage the children to brush with up and down strokes and in circles. Have them dip their brushes in water as necessary. Explain that just as brushing the tiles gets the food off the tiles, brushing their teeth after every meal cleans the food off their teeth and keeps them healthy.

Happy Tooth, Sad Tooth

Cut pictures of high-sugar foods and healthy low-sugar foods out of old magazines. Cover them with clear self-stick paper for durability, if desired. Make two boxes for sorting the pictures, one with a happy tooth shape on it and one with a sad tooth shape on it. Show the boxes to the children. Talk about why certain kinds of foods would make teeth "happy" or "sad." Then let the children sort the pictures into the boxes, putting the pictures of low-sugar foods in the happy tooth box and the pictures of high-sugar foods in the sad tooth box.

I Brush My Teeth

Sung to: "Jingle Bells"

I brush my teeth, I brush my teeth,
Morning, noon, and night.
I brush them, floss them, rinse them clean,
I keep them nice and white.
I brush them once, I brush them twice,
I brush them till they shine.
I always brush them up and down,
Those precious teeth of mine.

I eat good foods, I eat good foods,
I give my teeth a treat.
I always eat fruits, breads and milk,
Vegetables and meat.
If I eat sweets, if I eat sweets,
I brush right away
To keep my teeth shiny bright,
And free from tooth decay.

Stella Waldron
Lincoln, NE

Little Tommy Toothbrush

Sung to: "Eensy, Weensy Spider"

Little Tommy Toothbrush
Had a big job to do.
He spread himself with toothpaste
And jumped up on a tooth.
He scrubbed and scrubbed the germs away
To prevent tooth decay.
Then Little Tommy Toothbrush
Jumped down and said, "Hooray!"

Pat Cook
Hartford, VT

Apple Rounds

Ask the children why they think that apples are said to be "nature's toothbrushes." Then let them help you prepare this apple snack. Core several apples. Fill each one with soft cheese or peanut butter. Slice the apples into rounds and serve.

Children's Books:
- *Arthur's Tooth*, Marc Brown, (Little, Brown, 1985).
- *Bear's Toothache*, David McPhail, (Viking, 1972).
- *Little Rabbit's Loose Tooth*, Lucy Bate, (Crown, 1975).

Contributors:
Paula Schneider, Kent, WA
Anne Lemay Zipf, Metuchen, NJ

Paper Collages

Discuss with the children how paper is made from trees. Help them to think of all the different kinds of paper they use. Let the children each draw a picture of a tree in the center of a large piece of construction paper. Then set out different kinds of paper for them to tear into pieces and glue around their trees in collage form. Use wrapping paper, tissue paper, wallpaper, newspaper, waxed paper, food wrappers, paper bags, facial tissues, envelopes, etc.

Four Seasons

A deciduous tree looks different in each season. Help the children to understand this by having them make trees, one for every season. For each child you will need four empty toilet tissue tubes and two paper plates. Cut two slits, directly opposite each other, in one end of each of the toilet tissue tubes. Cut the paper plates in half. Have the children each paint their four toilet tissue tubes brown. Then have them use crayons or felt-tip markers to decorate one of their paper plate halves with blossoms, one with green leaves, one with red and orange leaves and one with bare tree branches. When they have finished, help them insert their paper plate halves in the slits in their toilet tissue tubes to complete their trees.

Plant-A-Forest Game

Paint a shoebox brown and cut six slits in the lid of the box. Number the slits from 1 to 6. Cut six tree shapes out of green construction paper and attach them to Popsicle sticks. Number the trees from 1 to 6. To play the game, have the children identify the numbers on the trees and insert them into the matching numbered slits in the shoebox lid.

Tree Game

Cut a bare tree shape out of brown felt. Mount the tree on cardboard or place it on a flannelboard. Then cut out ten to twenty small felt leaf shapes. Have the children take turns putting different numbers of leaves on the tree. Count the leaves each time as you remove them.

Variation: Use a felt-tip marker to color a long white glove brown. Attach loops of masking tape (sticky sides out) to the backs of the felt leaf shapes. Slip on the glove to turn your hand and arm into a "tree" and let the children attach the leaves to the finger "branches."

Wood Sort

In a box put a variety of small items made from wood and a variety of small items made from other materials. Have the children sort the items into two groups.

Trees in a Row

Let the children use their trees from the "Four Seasons" activity on page 242 to play a sequencing game. Have them try lining up their trees in the order of the seasons, starting with a different season each time.

Trees

Sung to: "The Farmer in the Dell"

The trees are growing high,
 (Raise arms overhead, fingers touching.)
The trees are growing high.
With soil and rain and sunny days,
The trees are growing high.

The trees are growing roots,
 (Bend over and touch floor.)
The trees are growing roots.
With soil and rain and sunny days,
The trees are growing roots.

The trees are growing bark,
 (Run hands up and down sides.)
The trees are growing bark.
With soil and rain and sunny days,
The trees are growing bark.

Additional verses: "The trees are growing branches;
The trees are growing leaves."

Susan Peters
Upland, CA

Tree Charades

On index cards draw pictures of things you can do in a tree (climb, pick apples, etc.); under a tree (rake leaves, pick up pinecones, etc.); and with a tree (decorate it, chop it up for firewood, etc.). Have one child choose a card and show it to the others. Then have all the children act out the activity pictured on the card.

Tree Treats

Let the children taste a variety of foods that grow on trees. Set out foods such as apples, pears, bananas, oranges or other fruits; walnuts, hazelnuts, pecans or other nuts; olives; and chocolate (which is made from the seeds of the cacao tree).

Children's Books:
- *Apple Tree Christmas*, Trinka Noble, (Dial, 1984).
- *Little Fir Tree*, Margaret Wise Brown, (Harper, 1985).
- *Real Hole*, Beverly Cleary, (Morrow, 1986).

Contributors:
Susan Peters, Upland, CA

Paper Bag Turkeys

Give each child a brown paper grocery bag (any size) and several sheets of newspaper. Have the children crumple the sheets of newspaper and stuff them into their bags until the bags are half full. Twist the bags closed and tie them around the middle with pieces of yarn. To make tails for their paper bag turkeys, have the children make several cuts from the top edges of their bags down to the yarn ties. Let the children paint their turkey tails, using bright autumn colors. Then give each child a precut turkey head shape to decorate. Attach the head shapes to the fronts of the bags to complete the turkeys.

Paper Collage Turkeys

Cut turkey shapes out of brown construction paper. Give each child a turkey shape and scraps of colorful construction paper. Let the children tear the construction paper into small pieces. Have them glue the torn pieces on their turkey shapes to make colored feathers. Then let them use felt-tip markers to add eyes and other features.

Turkeys in the Barnyard

Have the children paint their fingers and palms brown and their thumbs red. Then have them press their hands on a large sheet of butcher paper to make "turkey" prints. After the paint has dried, let the children add eyes, beaks, legs and feet with felt-tip markers. Hang the paper on a wall or bulletin board. Add barnyard shapes cut from construction paper (a large red barn, a fence, etc.) to make a barnyard mural.

My Turkey

As you recite the poem below, have the children act out the movements described.

I have a turkey, big and fat.
He spreads his wings
    (Fan hands at hips.)
And walks like that.
    (Struts back and forth.)
His daily corn he would not miss,
    (Pretend to eat corn.)
And when he talks, he sounds like this —
Gobble, gobble, gobble.

Dee Hoffman, Judy Panko
Aitkin, MN

TURKEYS

Five Little Turkeys

Cut five turkey shapes out of brown felt. Cut feather shapes out of other colors of felt and glue them to the turkey shapes. Place all of the turkey shapes on a flannelboard. Remove one shape at a time as you recite the poem below.

Five little turkeys by the barn door,
One waddled off, then there were four.

Four little turkeys out under the tree,
One waddled off, then there were three.

Three little turkeys with nothing to do,
One waddled off, then there were two.

Two little turkeys in the noonday sun,
One waddled off, then there was one.

One little turkey — better run away!
Soon will come Thanksgiving Day.

Jean Warren

Turkey Feather Game

Cut five turkey body shapes out of brown felt and fifteen feather shapes out of red, yellow and orange felt. Number the turkey body shapes from 1 to 5 and put them on a flannelboard. Place the feather shapes in a pile. To play the game, have the children take turns selecting a turkey, identifying the number on it and adding that many feathers to it.

Pin the Feather on the Turkey

Draw a picture of a featherless turkey on a large piece of poster-board. Attach the picture to a wall. Put loops of masking tape (sticky sides out) on the backs of real or paper feathers and place the feathers on a table close to the turkey picture. Have the children take turns choosing a feather from the table and then closing their eyes while they try to "pin" the feather on the turkey. (The crazy placement of all the feathers adds to the fun.)

Turkey Strut

Use pieces of masking tape to make turkey footprints all over the floor. Start playing some music. Let the children pretend to be turkeys and strut around the room. When you stop the music, have the turkeys find footprints to stand on (one turkey to a footprint). When you start the music again, have the turkeys continue strutting around the room.

Stuff the Turkey

Make a "turkey" by opening a large grocery bag and rolling down the top edges three or four times. Place the bag on the floor, open end up. Stuff the bottom halves of two small lunch sacks with newspaper, fasten the tops with twist ties and mold them into turkey leg shapes. Attach the leg shapes to the sides of the large bag. Give the children 6-inch squares of newspaper. Let them take turns "stuffing the turkey" by crumpling the newspaper squares and tossing them into the large grocery bag turkey.

Hello, Mr. Turkey

Sung to: "If You're Happy and You Know It"

Hello, Mr. Turkey, how are you?
Hello, Mr. Turkey, how are you?
With a gobble, gobble, gobble,
And a wobble, wobble, wobble.
Hello, Mr. Turkey, how are you?

Barbara H. Jackson
Denton, TX

Graham Cracker Turkeys

Combine in a blender ¼ cup unsweetened frozen apple juice concentrate, ¼ cup vegetable oil, 1 sliced banana, 1 teaspoon vanilla and 1 teaspoon cinnamon. In a large bowl, mix together 1 cup graham flour, 1 cup whole-wheat flour, ½ teaspoon baking soda and ½ teaspoon salt. Add the apple juice mixture to the flour mixture and stir thoroughly. Roll out the dough on a floured surface and cut out turkey shapes with a cookie cutter. Using a fork, poke holes in the turkeys to make eyes and feathers. Bake at 350 degrees for 8 minutes. Serve the turkey crackers plain or let the children spread them with peanut butter. Makes 2 to 3 dozen turkeys.

Children's Books:
- *Arthur's Thanksgiving*, Marc Brown, (Little Brown, 1983).
- *Farmer Goff and His Turkey Sam*, Brian Schatell, (Harper, 1982).
- *Sometimes It's Turkey, Sometimes It's Feathers*, Lorna Balian, (Abingdon, 1986).

Turkey Fruit Cups

For each child scoop out the center of an orange half (cut first along the inside of the rind). Dice the orange segments, ¼ of an apple and ¼ of a banana and combine the pieces in a small bowl. If desired, add chopped nuts. Fill the orange cup with the diced fruit. Add a toothpick for a neck, a round carrot slice for a head and half a toothpick for a beak. Stick 2 celery leaves in the back of the cup for feathers. Place a lettuce leaf on a plate to make a leafy bed for the fruit cup turkey.

Note: Have the children remove the toothpicks before eating their fruit cup turkeys.

Contributors:
Linda Kaman, R.S.M., Pittsburgh, PA
Joleen Meier, Marietta, GA
Betty Silkunas, Lansdale, PA

Droplet Designs

Fill several cups with water and add food coloring. Give each child an eyedropper and a piece of fabric or absorbent paper such as a coffee filter or a paper towel. Then let the children use their eyedroppers to drop colored water on their fabric or papers. Have them observe as the water evaporates, leaving only the color on the absorbent material.

Splatter Paintings

Have the children paint designs on construction paper with different colors of tempera paint. While the paintings are still wet, take them outside. Let the children splatter water on their paintings with small watering cans (or use spray bottles). Have the children watch as the colors on their paintings run and mix together.

Paint Washes

Have the children use crayons to draw pictures on construction paper. Make a paint wash by diluting tempera paint with water. Then let the children brush the paint wash over their papers to make the crayon drawings stand out.

Evaporation

Let the children observe the process of evaporation by hanging wet clothes on a line to dry, leaving a bowl of water on a windowsill for several days or by drying fruits. Evaporation occurs when particles of water become warm enough to escape into the air. Discuss with the children where the water goes. Can they think of ways to make water evaporate faster?

Making Sounds

Fill four glasses with different levels of water. Carefully strike each glass with a spoon. Each glass will make a different sound. Challenge the children to listen for the differences. Which sound is the highest? Which sound is the lowest? When water is added or removed from a glass, how does the sound change?

Absorption

Give each child an eyedropper, a small cup of water and a variety of absorbent and non-absorbent materials such as newspaper, waxed paper, paper towels, paper napkins, rubber, wool, cotton and plastic. Have each child select one material at a time, drop water on it and observe whether or not the water is absorbed. Then ask the children to sort the materials into two groups, one containing materials that absorb water, the other containing materials that don't.

Plants and Water

Plants need water to grow. To demonstrate, purchase two identical plants. Water one plant but not the other. Let the children observe what happens.

Capillary Action

Split a stalk of celery up the middle, almost to the leaves. Fill two glasses with water and add red food coloring to one glass and blue food coloring to the other. Set up the celery stalk with one half in the red water and one half in the blue. Let the children observe over a period of several hours as the colored water rises up the celery stalk and turns the leaves red and blue.

I Live in the Water

Discuss with the children animals that live in the water and animals that don't. Then say the name of an animal. If the animal lives in the water, have the children clap their hands. If the animal doesn't live in water, have them keep their hands in their laps.

Variation: Instead of clapping, have the children make swimming motions whenever they hear the name of an animal that lives in water.

Water Charades

Make cards that have pictures of different activities you can do in or with water, such as swimming, brushing teeth and watering plants. Sitting in a group, ask one child to draw a card and without showing it to anyone, act out the movement pictured on the card. Once the other children have guessed the activity, let another child draw a card. Continue until each child has had a turn.

We're So Lucky to Have Water

Sung to: "Mary Had a Little Lamb"

We're so lucky to have water,
To have water, to have water.
We're so lucky to have water,
We can wash our faces with it.

Repeat, letting the children take turns
naming other things they can do with
water.

Jean Woods
Tulsa, OK

Children's Books:
• *Little Island*, Golden Macdonald,
  (Doubleday, 1946).
• *Maggie B.*, Irene Haas,
  (Macmillan, 1975).
• *Noah's Ark*, Peter Spier,
  (Doubleday, 1977).

Snacktime

Take advantage of snacktime to
demonstrate and discuss what
happens when water is boiled,
frozen, evaporated and used to
dilute. For example: boil water to
make hard-boiled eggs or noodles;
freeze water to make Popsicles or
ice cubes with fruit pieces inside;
dry fruits to demonstrate evaporation; dilute juice concentrate with
water to make fruit juice.

Contributors:
Marjorie Debowy, Stony Brook, NY
Nancy C. Windes, Denver, CO

WATERMELONS

Watermelon Art

Give each child a circle cut out of green construction paper and a slightly smaller circle cut out of red construction paper. Have the children glue their red circles on top of their green ones. Then let them glue watermelon seeds all over their red circles.

Planting Watermelon Seeds

Let the children spoon potting soil into egg cartons. Have them plant one or two watermelon seeds in each section. Then let them water their seeds and check them daily. Soon the seeds will sprout and grow into small watermelon plants.

Watermelon Weighing

Buy a few different sized watermelons and let the children weigh them. Have the children compare the weights and sizes of the melons.

What Am I?

Cut a large circle out of green felt, a slightly smaller circle out of white felt, a still smaller circle out of red felt and several seed shapes out of black felt. Place the felt shapes in front of a flannelboard. As you read the poem below, put the appropriate shapes on the flannelboard.

Great big green ball
Sitting in the sun.
Inside, a white ball
Just for fun.

Next comes a red ball
Just for me,
Filled with black spots.
What can it be?

Black spots, black spots,
Spit 'em at the sun.
Spitting black spots
Is lots of fun.

Red ball, red ball,
Juicy and sweet.
Watch out now
While I eat and eat.

White ball, white ball,
Green ball, too.
I throw them away
When I'm through.

Can you guess
What I'm tellin'?
My great big ball
Is a watermelon!

Jean Warren

Watermelon Slices

Draw from one to ten watermelon slices on ten white index cards. Write the numbers 1 to 10 on ten other index cards. Mix up the cards and let the children take turns matching the numbers with the pictures.

WATERMELONS

The Watermelon Song
Sung to: ''Frere Jacques''

Watermelon, watermelon,
Tastes so yummy, tastes so yummy.
Green on the outside,
Red on the inside,
With black seeds, with black seeds.

Ellen Javernick
Loveland, CO

Picking Up Watermelons
Sung to: ''The Paw Paw Patch''

Pick up a watermelon, put it in the basket,
Pick up a watermelon, put it in the basket,
Pick up a watermelon, put it in the basket,
Way down yonder in the watermelon patch.

Have the children pretend to pick up watermelons
and place them in a basket while singing the song.

Jean Warren

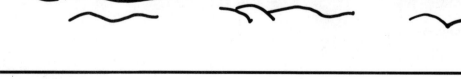

Giant Fruit Cup

Have the children help make a huge fruit cup. Let them scoop out the insides of a watermelon, remove the seeds and set the fruit aside. Help them cut up other fruits such as apples, oranges, bananas and grapes. Then let them mix the fruit chunks with the scooped-out watermelon and spoon the fruit mixture back into the watermelon shell.

Watermelon Popsicles

Blend 1 cup seedless watermelon chunks, 1 cup orange juice and 1 cup water in a blender. Pour into small paper cups. Place in freezer and when partially frozen, insert small plastic spoons for handles. When completely frozen, pour hot water over the bottoms of the cups to remove the frozen treats.

Children's Books:
- *Picnic*, Emily McCully, (Harper, 1984).
- *Relatives Came*, Cynthia Rylant, (Bradbury, 1985).

Contributors:
Betty Loew White, Columbus, OH

WORMS

Worm Tracks

Let the children dip 6-inch pieces of string into brown tempera paint. Have them pull the strings across pieces of construction paper to make "worm tracks." Encourage them to make their strings crawl and wiggle like real worms.

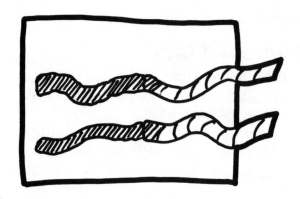

Worm Collages

Mix red, yellow and blue food coloring together to make brown. Add drops of the brown food coloring to cooked drained spaghetti to create "worms." Let the children arrange the worms on paper plates or Styrofoam food trays. (The starch in the spaghetti will act as glue.)

Worm Finger Puppets

Set out small paper cups and squares of brown tissue paper or construction paper. Help each child make a finger-sized hole in the bottom of a cup. Then let the children tear the brown paper into tiny pieces and use them to fill their cups half full. To work the puppets, have the children stick their index fingers up through the holes in the bottoms of their cups and wiggle them like worms.

Willie Worm

Have the children hold their worm finger puppets as described in the activity on this page. Have them keep their index fingers hidden under the torn paper in their cups while you recite the poem below. At the end of the poem, have them poke their fingers up out of the paper and wiggle them.

I have a pet named Willie,
Who lives at home with me.
I keep him in this special cup,
So all my friends can see.

Where, oh, where is Willie?
Oh, where can Willie be?
Come out now, little Willie,
So all my friends can see.

He is a little timid,
I must be very firm.
Come out now, little Willie!
Come out, my Willie Worm!

Jean Warren

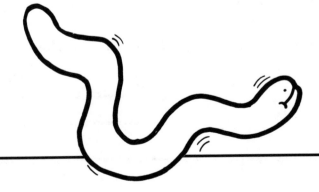

WORMS

Observing Earthworms

Place an earthworm on top of some soil for the children to observe. Ask: "How does the earthworm move? What color is it? What does its skin look like? What does its skin feel like? What do you suppose the worm does in the soil?" Explain that earthworms hatch from eggs that are inside a cocoon in the soil. The worms are very tiny when they are born and many worms hatch from one cocoon. The only facial feature an earthworm has is a mouth through which soil (an earthworm's food) enters. Little piles of an earthworm's digested soil can be found near the opening of the worm's tunnel. These are called "castings."

Earthworm Farm

Fill a wooden frame with earthworm bedding material purchased from a sporting goods store. (Or make your own bedding material by mixing potting soil with sphagnum moss and a sprinkling of cornmeal.) Add worms you have collected from other locations. To feed the worms, dust the bedding material with cornmeal from time to time.

Finger Worms

Cut five apple shapes (approximately 5- by 5-inches) out of cardboard or posterboard. Cut one hole (large enough for a child's finger to pass through) in the first apple, two holes in the second apple and so on. Write the numeral that matches the number of holes on the front of each apple. Let the children help color the apples red. Then have them choose apples, stick fingers through the holes and tell how many ''worms'' they see.

Earthworm Hunt

Take the children on a nature walk to search for earthworms. Before going on the walk, locate a garden or a compost pile where there are many worms or ''seed'' a small prepared area with worms you have found in other places. (If necessary, check with a sporting goods store to find out where earthworms can be purchased in your area.) When you reach your selected site, use a spade to turn over the soil and let the children look for worms. Put the worms in a plastic container with enough damp soil to cover them. Then take the worms back to use for other activities in this unit.

WORMS

Worm Puzzle

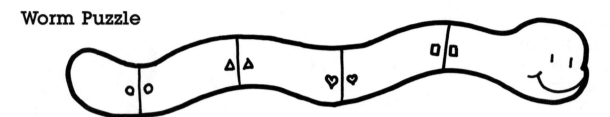

Cut a large curvy worm shape out of posterboard. Then cut the shape into six sections to make a worm puzzle. To help the children put the puzzle together, glue or draw matching shapes, colors, numbers, etc., on either side of each cut line. Cover the puzzle pieces with clear self-stick paper, if desired.

Wiggle Worm
Sung to: "Did You Ever See a Lassie?"

Did you ever see a wiggle worm,
A wiggle worm, a wiggle worm?
Did you ever see a wiggle worm
Move this way and that?
Move this way and that way,
Move this way and that way.
Did you ever see a wiggle worm
Move this way and that?

Have the children wiggle their fingers, arms or entire bodies as they sing the song.

Betty Silkunas
Lansdale, PA

Giant Worm Pretzels

Dissolve 1 package yeast in 1½ cups warm water (105 to 115 degrees) and add ½ teaspoon sugar. Then add 4½ cups flour and knead for six minutes. Let dough rise, covered, in a greased bowl until double in size. Divide dough into 12 pieces and let the children roll them into long ''worm'' shapes. Blend together 1 egg yolk and 2 tablespoons water and have the children brush some of the mixture on their pretzel ''worms.'' Next let them sprinkle on some coarse salt or sesame seeds, if desired. Help them lay their ''worms'' on a cookie sheet and bake at 450 degrees for 12 minutes.

Children's Books:
• *Inch by Inch*, Leo Lionni, (Knopf, 1960).

Contributors:
Lois Olson, Webster City, IA
Betty Loew White, Columbus, OH

Sewing With Yarn

Use a hole punch to punch holes around the edges of paper plates. Give each child a plastic needle with a piece of yarn threaded through it. (Plastic needles are available at craft stores.) Show the children how to use their needles and yarn to "sew" around their plates.

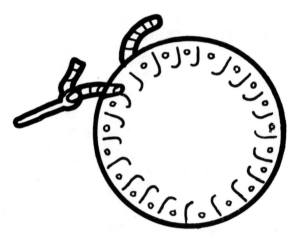

Yarn Bubbles

Blow up a small balloon for each child. Mix equal parts of liquid starch and glue together in Styrofoam food trays. Cut different colors of yarn into long pieces. Let the children dip the yarn pieces into the starch and glue mixture and wrap them around their balloons. Hang the balloons to dry. When the yarn has completely dried, pop the balloons and carefully remove them.

Dyeing Yarn

Put different colors of food coloring into clear plastic cups and add small amounts of water. Give the children 6-inch pieces of thick white yarn. Ask the children to guess what will happen when they put their yarn into the food coloring. Then have them dip their yarn pieces into the different colors of "dye." Allow the yarn pieces to dry on sheets of newspaper, then let the children sort them by color.

Yarn Day

Have the children bring things from home that have been made from yarn. Let each child talk about his or her item. Ask the children to describe the different colors, textures and uses of the articles they have brought.

Yarn Circle Fun

Give each child a 4-foot piece of yarn. Show the children how to form large circles on the floor with their pieces of yarn. Then ask the children to follow directions such as these: "Place your right foot inside your circle; Place your left elbow inside your circle; Jump into your circle; Walk around your circle."

Color Bracelets

Use small pieces of green, yellow, red and blue yarn to make bracelets. Place the yarn bracelets in a bucket. Let each child take a colored bracelet out of the bucket, name the color and slip it over his or her wrist. Then have the children sit in a circle. Ask them to listen carefully as you sing the song below and to raise their hands when they hear the color names of the bracelets they are wearing.

Sung to: "If You're Happy and You Know It"

If you're wearing green today,
Raise your hand.
If you're wearing yellow today,
Raise your hand.
If you're wearing red today,
Then raise your hand — hurray!
If you're wearing blue today,
Raise your hand.

Repeat, each time changing the order of the color names.

Gayle Bittinger

Yarn Shapes

Use glue and pieces of yarn to create a different shape on each of five index cards. Draw matching shapes with felt-tip markers on five additional index cards. Give the cards to the children and let them take turns finding the matching pairs of shapes.

Mary Had a Wooly Lamb
Sung to: "Mary Had a Little Lamb"

Mary had a wooly lamb,
Wooly lamb, wooly lamb.
Mary had a wooly lamb,
Its wool was white as snow.

Its wool got thick and very heavy,
Very heavy, very heavy.
Its wool got thick and very heavy,
So its fleece was sheared.

The wool was soon made into yarn,
Into yarn, into yarn.
The wool was soon made into yarn,
And woven into cloth.

Now Mary has a wooly coat,
Wooly coat, wooly coat.
Now Mary has a wooly coat,
That she wears to school.

Jean Warren

Children's Books:
- *Charlie Needs a Cloak,* Tomie De Paola, (Prentice Hall, 1974).
- *A New Coat for Anna,* Harriet Ziefert, (Knopf, 1986).
- *Patchwork Quilt,* Valerie Flournoy, (Dial, 1985).

Contributors:
Susan M. Paprocki, Northbrook, IL
Susan Peters, Upland, CA

Zebra Masks

Give each child a paper plate with eye holes cut out of the center. Let the children paint vertical black stripes on the backs of their plates to make zebra faces. When the paint has dried, have the children glue on precut black construction paper nose and ear shapes. (To prevent smears, have them glue their ear shapes to the unpainted sides of their masks.) Display the finished masks on a wall or a bulletin board. Or attach tongue depressors for handles and let the children use their masks for dramatic play.

Black and White Mural

Collect several empty roll-on deodorant bottles. Remove the rollers from the bottles and wash the rollers and the bottles thoroughly. Fill the bottles with black tempera paint and replace the rollers. Put a large piece of white butcher paper on the floor. Give the children the paint-filled deodorant bottles and let them work together to create a black and white mural.

Where Do Zebras Live?

Explain to the children that zebras live on the plains of Africa. Zebras live there because they like to eat the grasses and drink the water from the rivers and lakes that are there. Show pictures from books of the African plains as well as picture of other environments (cities, mountains, tropical forests, snow-covered landscapes, etc.). As you hold up each picture, ask the children to clap if they think that zebras would like to live in such a place.

Galloping Zebras

Have the children stand in a large circle and pretend to be zebras. Select one child to sit in the middle of the circle and beat out fast and slow rhythms on a drum. Let the zebras gallop around the circle to the rhythms of the drum.

Nine Little Zebras

Cut nine zebra shapes out of white felt and use a black felt-tip marker to add stripes. Place the zebra shapes on a flannelboard one at a time and then remove them as you read the poem below.

One little, two little, three little zebras,
Four little, five little, six little zebras,
Seven little, eight little, nine little zebras,
Galloping across the plain.

Nine little, eight little, seven little zebras,
Six little, five little, four little zebras,
Three little, two little, one little zebra,
Galloping back again.

Jean Warren

Stripe Matching

Draw from one to five black stripes on five pairs of index cards. Mix up the cards and let the children take turns matching the stripes.

Black and White Sort

Cut several shapes out of black construction paper. Then cut matching shapes out of white construction paper. Give the shapes to the children and let them take turns sorting them by color or by shape.

I'm a Little Zebra

Sung to: "I'm a Little Teapot"

I'm a little zebra, white and black,
Big bushy mane riding down my back.
I like to gallop and run and play
Out on the African plains all day.

Jean Warren

Black and White Sandwiches

To make 4 finger sandwiches, cut the crusts off 2 slices of white bread. Spread each slice with softened cream cheese. Sprinkle chopped black olives on top of 1 slice and put the other slice on top of that. Cut lengthwise into 4 rectangles.

Children's Books:
• *Greedy Zebra,* Mwenye Hadithi, (Little, Brown, 1984).

INDEX

INDEX

Activities, songs and new ideas
to use right now are waiting for you
in every issue of the TOTLINE newsletter.

Each issue puts the fun into teaching with 24 pages of challenging and creative activities for young children, including open-ended art activities, learning games, music, language and science activities.

Sample issue $1 • One year subscription $15 (6 issues)

Beautiful bulletin boards, games
and flannelboards are easy
with PRESCHOOL PATTERNS.

You won't want to miss a single issue of PRESCHOOL PATTERNS with 3 large sheets of patterns delightfully and simply drawn. Each issue includes patterns for making flannelboard characters, bulletin boards, learning games and more!

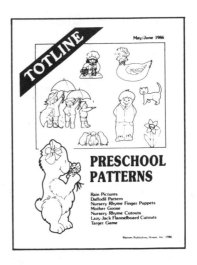

Sample issue $2 • One year subscription $18 (6 issues)

ORDER FROM:
Totline • P.O. Box 2255, Dept. B • Everett, WA 98203

Totline Books

Super Snacks – 120 seasonal sugarless snack recipes kids love.

Teaching Tips – 300 helpful hints for working with young children.

Teaching Toys – over 100 toy and game ideas for teaching learning concepts.

Piggyback Songs – 110 original songs, sung to the tunes of childhood favorites.

More Piggyback Songs – 195 more original songs.

Piggyback Songs for Infants and Toddlers – 160 original songs, for infants and toddlers.

Piggyback Songs in Praise of God – 185 original religious songs, sung to familiar tunes.

Piggyback Songs in Praise of Jesus – 240 more original religious songs.

Holiday Piggyback Songs – over 240 original holiday songs.

1-2-3 Art – over 200 open-ended art activities.

1-2-3 Games – 70 no-lose games for ages 2 to 8.

1-2-3 Colors – over 500 Color Day activities for young children.

Teeny-Tiny Folktales – 15 folktales from around the world plus flannelboard patterns.

Short-Short Stories – 18 original stories plus seasonal activities.

Mini-Mini Musicals – 10 simple musicals, sung to familiar tunes.

Small World Celebrations – 16 holidays from around the world to celebrate with young children.

"Cut & Tell" Scissor Stories for Fall – 8 original stories plus patterns.

"Cut & Tell" Scissor Stories for Winter – 8 original stories plus patterns.

"Cut & Tell" Scissor Stories for Spring – 8 original stories plus patterns.

Seasonal Fun – 50 two-sided reproducible parent flyers.

Theme-A-Saurus – the great big book of mini teaching themes.

Check your local school supply store for these outstanding books or write for our FREE catalog.

Warren Publishing House, Inc. • P.O. Box 2255, Dept. B • Everett, WA 98203